MARCO ⊕ POLO

W9-CDA-533

Vienna

With **Insider Tips**

This travel guide was written by Walter
M. Weiss, a freelance author living in
Vienna. He became known above all for his
publications on Austrian cultural history.
For further detailed information, see
www.wmweiss.com

marcopolo.de
The latest insider tips can be found at
www.marcopolo.de, see also page 103

MAIRS GEOGRAPHISCHER VERLAG

Insider Tip

MARCO POLO INSIDER TIPS:
Discovered for you by our author

★ **MARCO POLO HIGHLIGHTS:**
Vienna top tips at a glance

SITES WITH A SCENIC VIEW

PLACES WHERE YOUNG PEOPLE GET TOGETHER

PRICE CATEGORIES

Hotels	
€€€	over 110 Euro
€€	80–110 Euro
€	under 80 Euro

Prices are for two people sharing a double room including breakfast.

Restaurants	
€€€	over 18 Euro
€€	11–18 Euro
€	under 11 Euro

Prices are for a starter, main course and dessert, drinks not included.

MAPS

[110 A1] Page numbers and coordinates for the Vienna Street Atlas

A plan of the U- and S-Bahn networks can be found inside back cover.

Overview map of Vienna and surrounding area on pages 126–127

For your orientation, coordinates are also given for places which are not marked in the Street Atlas.

DID YOU KNOW?

CONTENTS

The most important
MARCO POLO **Highlights**
Sights and sounds you can't afford to miss

 Kaisergruft
Final resting place of the Habsburgs since the 17th century (page 21)

 Belvedere
Baroque at its best in Prince Eugene's two summer palaces. With Klimt, Schiele & Co. into the bargain at the Austrian Gallery (page 22, 46)

 Hofburg
Once the residence of the Habsburgs – including treasure chamber, choirboys and Lipizzaner (page 24)

 Schloss Schönbrunn
A tour of the magnificent chambers of the Habsburg summer residence should include a walk around the extensive palace gardens (page 27)

 Stephansdom
Guided tour of Vienna's No. 1 landmark, the Gothic cathedral. Plus a climb up the tower with its fabulous view (page 33)

 Prater
Woods, meadows, 'Wurstelprater' and ferris wheel – the recreational paradise with its own U-Bahn link (page 35)

Fun for young and old in the amusement park 'Wurstelprater'

Heuriger wine tavern in Grinzing

Fiacre at the Hofburg

 The highlights are marked on the map on the back cover

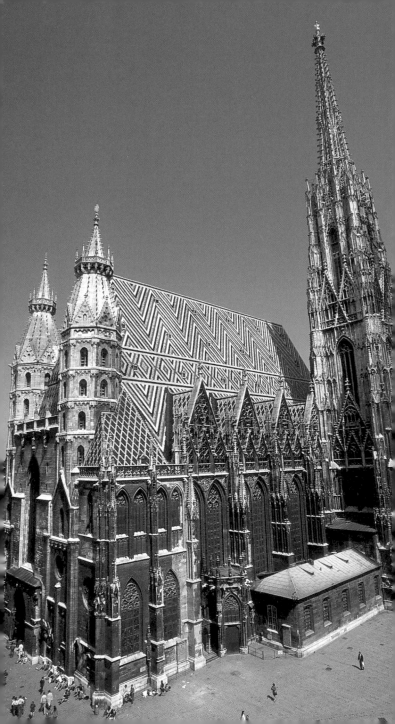

Discover Vienna!

Rich in tradition, the capital city and once royal seat is a marriage between a glorious past and a lively present

Old and new: fiacre and tram

Vienna is different. This slogan has long been used to attract visitors from home and abroad to Austria's federal capital – though occasionally it only gave rise to some head scratching. This curious theory, however, has more than just a grain of truth in it to this day, in many respects.

Vienna really is different now, compared to the end of the 1960s and beginning of the 1970s. At that time, it had the air of an ageing screen goddess. A pretty morbid place with grey, crumbling façades, grumpy elderly residents and, in the evenings, streets which were as quiet as a grave. Today, on the other hand, the bright and cheerful former imperial city welcomes its guests in fine style. Whether on Heldenplatz in front of the imperial backdrop of the Hofburg, in the revitalised Biedermeier quarters in the former suburbs, in the wide stopping streets or new ecological housing estates on the periphery: Vienna exudes optimism, prosperity and zest for life. The transformation began in the mid-1970s. The city-

The venerable Gothic St. Stephen's Cathedral is the symbol of Vienna

scape and infrastructure were given a complete make-over. This included the opening of Vienna's first U-Bahn line in 1978. A sizeable proportion of the largely ramshackle buildings from past centuries was renovated. Not only buildings of cultural and historical value such as the Hofburg, the Karlskirche and the Belvedere, but also smaller churches and city palaces shone once again. Contemporary architecture, too, was also able to distinguish itself in a number of showpiece projects, the most notable without a doubt being the Haas House on Stephansplatz. 1979 saw the opening of UN City, making Vienna, after New York and Geneva, the third seat of the United Nations.

The 1970s also brought with them new cultural impetus. A

Angelic Voices

Vienna's living cultural treasure just gets younger all the time!

The Vienna Boys' Choir sings every Sunday from mid-September until the end of June, and also on Christmas Day during mass in the Chapel of the Imperial Palace at the Hofburg (entrance on Swiss Courtyard); they are accompanied by members of the choir and the orchestra of the State Opera. The service starts at 9.15 am. Tickets can be ordered in writing, at least ten weeks in advance from *Hofmusikkapelle; 1010 Vienna, Hofburg; Fax 01-533 99 27-75*. Last-minute tickets are obtainable on Fridays directly at the Chapel ticket office *(11 am–1 pm, 3 pm–5 pm)*. In addition, the boys can be heard every Friday at 4 pm from mid-April until mid-June, and in September and October at the Musikverein, where they sing to the music of Strauss and other Romantic composers. Tickets for these performances are available at hotels or via the travel agents *Reisebüro Mondial, Tel. 01-588 04-173 or -150*.

generously subsidised alternative cultural scene grew up, its countless small and medium-sized theatres calling into question the self-satisfied air of the existing old-established and highly sophisticated milieu. At the same time Vienna celebrated its first successes in the world of musicals. Soon afterwards, a fresh breeze even wafted through the traditional Burgtheater, thanks to its new director Claus Peymann. Parallel to this a lively bar and pub scene developed, originating in the so-called 'Bermuda Triangle' in the northeast of the city centre. Today, evening entertainment is to be had all over the inner city and beyond. The fall of the Iron Curtain in 1989 was a decisive factor in the revitalisation of Vienna. All at once, the former imperial seat was no longer on the periphery of the western world, but took on the role once again, as in the days of the monarchy, of cultural, political and also economic nerve centre linking East and West. The population grew due to immigration from the East to over 1.6 million again. The city, governed since time immemorial by the Social Democrats, received its most recent modernisation impulse upon Austria's entry into the EU in 1995.

What makes Vienna different can be seen when compared to other European capitals. The Viennese are proud of their particular take on life. Their easy-going nature and proverbial 'Schmäh', that is the ability to meet even sad situations with humour and wit, may be somewhat clichéed. However, you only have

> *The Viennese are proud of their particular take on life*

to mingle with the locals, merry with wine, holding forth on some topic or other in the traditional wine taverns, the 'Heuriger', or observe the regulars at one of the traditional cafés, chatting over a 'Mélange' or reading the newspaper, seemingly with all the time in the world, to realise how fitting these attributes still are.

> *An ideal place to relax is along the New Danube*

Vienna's differentness is also used to great effect when advertising seemingly profane things such as its air and water, its forests and river banks. In actual fact, the city offers an exemplary quality of life which is somewhat taken for granted by the locals. Vienna is, for example, surprisingly free of dust and smog. Its lush vegetation is to a large extent responsible for this fact: Prater, Lobau, Laaer Berg, Schönbrunn, the Lainzer Tiergarten, the extensive woodlands between the valley of the River Wien and the Leopoldsberg in the northwest and the numerous inner-city parks together make up almost 50 per cent of the 415 sq km municipal area. A feature of many songs and paintings, parts of the Vienna Woods serve to filter dirt particles and supply oxygen. This forest, in some places over 40 km wide, partly encloses Vienna to the west. A unique and ideal place to relax is along the New Danube. Particularly pretty and close to the city, its kilometres of river bank in hot weather and on summer evenings are as busy and bustling as any Mediterranean hotspot.

Another point in Vienna's favour is the high degree of security in public places. Since the opening of borders to the East, the city has admittedly become a playground for traffickers and drug dealers, money launderers and secret service operatives. It is still possible, nevertheless, to move around its streets safely, even late at night.

To a certain extent, Vienna's picturesque situation corresponds to the historical role it has played through its more than 2,000-year history. Between the eastern foothills of the Alps and the western

Kärntnerstrasse: Vienna's top shopping boulevard

Carpathian Mountains, d in a basin, its terraced ng gently down to the River Danube, Vienna was as much border stronghold against invading peoples – generally from the East – as it was meeting place. In Roman times it was the site of an important army camp, *Vindobona,* which helped to secure the Danube limes, the Empire's border with the Germanic lands. During the high Middle Ages the Babenberg family held court here. For the next 650 years the Habsburgs ruled their huge empire from Vienna. Twice, in 1529 and 1683, the Turks stormed the city, on both occasions to no avail. In the wake of all this, Austria rose to become a major continental power.

Vienna, eastern bastion of Christianity, whose suburbs suffered so much, particularly during the second siege, was re-built under Emperors Leopold I and Charles VI, and transformed into a splendid Baroque metropolis, with magnificent churches, palaces and government buildings. Emperor Franz Joseph I freed the city of its corset of ramparts and fortifications in 1857. In their place, he had the magnificent boulevard, the Ringstrasse, built instead. In the second half of the 19th century, the era of massive industrialisation, the old imperial city grew to be a modern metropolis – one of the largest in the world at the time. The population rose to its highest-ever level, over 2 million, in 1910.

The city had long since proved its status as a centre for international understanding and diplomacy – for example in 1814–15 at the famous Congress of Vienna at which Europe's statesmen re-drew the map of Europe in the aftermath of the Napoleonic wars – and celebrated in style. The enviable ability either to forget or to solve one's problems – as required – over champagne and in three-four time is something the Viennese have not lost to this day. At Carnival time, the calendar is still packed with opportunities to take to the dance floor. Whatever the occupation, whether chemist or coffee-house proprietor, butcher, huntsman or jurist, everyone joins in. The high point of the season is, of course, the Opera Ball, where high society comes together in tails and evening dresses at the 'Haus am Ring'.

Champagne and three-four time

Vienna's bridge-building capacity has always gone hand in hand with its fate as an intellectual and ethnic melting pot. In the course of the 19th century the cultures of central and eastern Europe intermingled in the city on the Danube. The result was that intense, creative atmosphere which went down in the history of ideas as 'Viennese Fin de Siècle'. In those days, the great coffee houses were the focal point of Europe's intelligentsia. Leading writers such as Hugo von Hofmannsthal, Franz Werfel and Josef Roth honed their linguistic talents; Egon Erwin Kisch and Karl Kraus crossed swords – on paper at least. Karl Lueger and Victor Adler polished up their party programmes, Bertolt Brecht and Leo Trotzki played chess and even Sigmund Freud regularly reviewed his theor-

Palm House in the gardens of Schloss Schönbrunn

ies by observing 'living specimens' over coffee! Today, you can still sense the remnants of this inspirational atmosphere at Griensteidl, Bräunerhof, Central and the other stalwarts of the Viennese coffeehouse tradition.

The intellectual and artistic creativity of the city is, in actual fact, as remarkable as ever. The round 2.5 million guests who pour into the city every year from abroad are here largely because of its rich cultural tradition. They come to the auditorium of the Musikverein or the opera, where the likes of Richard Strauss, Gustav Mahler and Herbert von Karajan were wont to conduct, to listen to the velvet tones of the Vienna Philharmonic. They make pilgrimages to the Beethoven, Schu-

> *Great coffee-house culture and velvet tones: Vienna is a creative city*

bert, Haydn and Lehár memorials or visit the City Park, where Johann Strauss junior, immortalised in stone and coated in gold leaf, strikes up a waltz on the violin. Yet music is just one side of Vienna.

Take a stroll along Ringstrasse, across Heldenplatz and through the medieval alleyways; go on a pilgrimage to the Gothic and Baroque churches, to the venerable theatres or the grandiose art galleries and magnificent palaces, such as the Belvedere and Schloss Schönbrunn. And don't forget to try a taste of the fresh wine at the Heuriger in Grinzing in the evening. Younger visitors can throw themselves into the inner-city hustle and bustle and dance the night away in the discos.

Habsburg myth and hip-hop generation

Past and present accompany your every step in Vienna

Architecture

As far as the cityscape is concerned, Vienna has two faces: one is the venerable city centre whose pleasantly old-fashioned outline is characterised by Gothic and Historicist towers, Baroque cupolas and a sea of shingle-roofed houses from the *Biedermeier* and *Gründerzeit* years. The other is the ultra-modern skyline which has been shooting up along and beyond the Danube for some years now, the second focal point of urban life. At break-neck speed and at a respectful distance to the old part of town, Andromeda and Millennium Towers, UN City and Austria-Center, the Donau-City residential park, the Tech Gate technology centre and a host of other office and residential blocks are proof of the immense dynamism of the former imperial city. Among the creators of the new city are such famous names as Hans Hollein, Gustav Peichl, Wilhelm Holzbauer, Harry Seidler and Coop Himmelblau.

Danube

For centuries, in contrast to the waltzing cliché, Vienna did not lie

The new face of Vienna on the Danube

on the beautiful blue Danube, but next to it. It was not until the end of the 19th century that the course of the – in actual fact greyish-brown – river was straightened and re dir ected closer to the city, whereupon it burst its banks. The truly intimate relationship between city and river was re-established in the 1970s, when, in order to avert the danger of flooding once and for all, a second river bed was excavated. In the process an island was created, 200 m wide and over 20 km long, which was declared a recreational area, a kind of gigantic 'inland Adriatic', which the Viennese have meanwhile become very fond of. Cyclists, hikers, joggers and skaters love the long asphalt paths. Boy scouts and immigrants with Balkan roots like to barbecue their weekend lunch at the specially laid out picnic areas on the river banks. Close by, anglers in quiet contemplation hope for a good catch. In summer this artificial 'natural' landscape is transformed into a central-European Majorca. Sun-worshippers hog the lawns and 40-km-worth of sand and pebble beaches, ply the waters in pedalos and on water skis, play street soccer, basketball and beach volleyball. After sunset the largely young clientele parties till dawn in the many restaurants, bars and discos of the entertainment mile 'Copa Cagrana', which takes its name from the nearby Kagran district.

Habsburg and Co.

It may have vanished from the political scene more than 80 years ago, but the myth surrounding this dynasty, which ruled an empire for over 600 years, is (almost) as real today as when the Emperor was alive and kicking. To appreciate this, you don't have to mingle with the thousands of tourists who push and shove their way round the imperial apartments every day. You only have to look at the shelves of any bookshop, with their dozens of biographies of Maria Theresia, Crown Prince Rudolf and Empress Elisabeth (Sisi). It is no coincidence that fresh flowers are always to be found in the imperial burial vault lying in front of several of the sarcophagi, including that of Elisabeth, the 100th anniversary of whose death was celebrated with much PR pomp in 1998. Not without reason do many of the company plaques in the nobler shopping streets still bear the emblem of 'Purveyors to the Im-

perial and Royal Court'; the Habsburg colours black and yellow are coming back with a vengeance at the souvenir shops on flags, sweets and T-shirts; many fiacre drivers still grow long side whiskers in an effort to resemble Emperor Franz Joseph. What is behind all this? Certainly a good deal of commercial calculation. For a small minority perhaps genuine political yearnings. For the majority of Viennese, on the other hand, just the sentiment they usually attach to all things past: posthumous glorification. What did satirist Helmut Qualtinger once remark? 'In Vienna you have to die before you can become famous. Once you're dead, you're as good as immortal.'

Multicultural Vienna

The contradictory nature of the Viennese heart is well demonstrated by its attitude towards 'foreigners' who currently make up around 18 per cent of the population. On the one hand, the xenophobic remarks of provocateur Jörg Haider and his FPÖ party have fallen on alarmingly fertile ground, particularly in the federal capital – until recently at least. However, the family tree of a dyed-in-the-wool citizen of Vienna, although he prefers to ignore the fact, generally contains a Hungarian uncle and a Bohemian grandmother. The city's telephone book is bursting with Stastnys, Swobodas and Vranitzkys. On the other hand, it is sufficient to take a look at Vienna's streets and markets to recognise the pragmatic tolerance with which the city integrates its immigrants. Greek and Turkish dealers peacefully sell olives and unleavened bread on neighbouring stands. Many Arabs and Iranians who came here to study medicine are now highly respected medical practitioners. And the families of those foreign workers who once poured in from Croatia, Serbia and Turkey are long since firmly established Viennese citizens, whose children have mastered the soft, extended vowels of the local dialect to a T. No wonder the Viennese are proud that, in relation to its population, no other European country absorbed so many Hungarians in 1956, so many Czechs in 1968 and so many refugees from the former Yugoslavia in the 1990s as Austria did. And that the majority of these newcomers felt able to call the capital its second home. And that the verbal or even physical abuse to which foreigners are subjected by mindless chauvinists – an everyday occurrence elsewhere – is to this day still rare in Vienna.

Music

For younger visitors to the city, Strauss waltzes and the State Opera may be rather old hat. In its capacity as a world music metropolis, however, Vienna need not be shy of the house and hip-hop generation. A top-class contemporary scene has established itself here too – you might say on the quiet. It all started in the 1970s with pop bards Wolfgang Ambros and Rainhard Fendrich, who admittedly still sounded very Viennese. In the 1980s, Falco made it to number one in the US charts, proving that there really was such a thing as rap, Austrian-style. In recent years, out of the blue, local sampling and remix heroes such as Kruder & Dorfmeister, Pulsinger & Tunakan, Makossa or The WAZ Experience have catapulted themselves into the international electronic heavens. Since then, there's hardly a foray into Viennese nightlife that doesn't end in one of the many bars and clubs which are currently springing up, to hear the off-the-wall sound creations of such star DJs – and the odd up-and-coming desperado – sending the crowds into a permanent state of rapture.

Drinking Water

You notice Vienna's high quality of life as soon as you turn on the tap. What comes out is not, in contrast to most big cities, some chlorine-rich, purified liquid from underground or even from the water-treatment plant. It is, for the most part, pleasant-tasting, crystal-clear spring water from Austria's mountainous regions. The Viennese owe this privilege to a geologist named Eduard Suess, who 130 years ago – despite hefty resistance from the public authorities – realised a visionary project: a water pipeline bringing this precious fluid to the city. It has flowed non-stop since 1873 from the Rax and Schneeberg areas, via 90 km of tunnels and aqueducts – and has kept down permanently the turnover of the mineral water producers.

Festivals and Events

The calendar of events goes from contemplative to off-the-wall – Vienna is always in season and there's something for everyone to enjoy

From the New Year's concert via the Festival Weeks, the highpoint of the cultural calendar, to the film festival 'Viennale' in late autumn; from the ball season via countless music festivals to the Advent markets and the big New Year's Eve party: there's no excuse for being bored in Vienna.

Vienna: more than a classic party

Public Holidays

1 Jan *New Year's Day;* **6 Jan** *Epiphany;* **Easter Monday;** **1 May** *Labour Day;* **Ascension Day; Whit Monday; Corpus Christi; 15 Aug** *Assumption;* **26 Oct** *National Holiday;* **1 Nov** *All Saints' Day;* **8 Dec** *Immaculate Conception;* **25 Dec, 26 Dec** *Christmas*

Events

January/February

1 January: *New Year's concert* with the Vienna Philharmonic Orchestra in the Golden Hall of the Musikverein; *Tel. 503 31 94-1*
Beginning of January–end of February: *Carnival and ball season.* More than 200 festive balls staged by various promoters in magnificent halls
Second half of January: *Resonanzen:* Festival of old music at the Konzerthaus; *ticket hotline: 24 20 02*

March–May

Holy Week/Easter weekend: *OsterKlang:* Top musicians, including the Vienna Philharmonic Orchestra, play contemplative and festive music; *ticket hotline: 427 17*
Mid-April–beginning of May: *Spring Festival* at the Konzerthaus: classical music on a cheerful note; *ticket hotline: 24 20 02*

May/June

Vienna City Marathon: From the Schönbrunn Palace to the Prater, amateurs rub shoulders with top-class athletes from home and abroad.
Beginning of May–mid-June: *Vienna Festival Weeks:* Mega-event with the latest stage art from all over the world, performed at

dozens of venues; *ticket reservations: Wiener Festwochen; 1060 Vienna, Lehárgasse 11; Tel. 589 22-22; by credit card: 589 22-11; Fax 589 22-49* Final weekend in June: *Danube Island Festival:* three-day giant party with music, sports shows and political cabaret

July–September

Beginning of July: *Jazz Festival:* Outdoors, in clubs and at the State Opera; *ticket hotline: 712 42 24* Beginning of July–mid-August. International Dance Weeks *Im-Puls:* the ultimate in 'physical art'; *ticket hotline: 523 55 58* Beginning of July–end of August: *Music Film Festival* in front of the City Hall: famous opera productions shown on big screens in the open air. Free admission, free choice of seats, food from market stalls Beginning of July–beginning of September: *KlangBogen:* around 150 operettas, operas, orchestra and chamber music concerts performed over two months – Vienna's musical summer at the most beautiful venues in the city; *ticket hotline: 427 17*

October

Viennale: Latest film creations from all over the globe; *Tel: 526 59 47-0* End of October: *Kunst Wien:* trade fair for contemporary art at the Museum of Applied Art (MAK); *Tel: 216 65 26-0* End of October–end of November: *Wien modern:* music of the 20th century at the Musikverein and Konzerthaus

November

Second half of the month: *Vienna Schubertiade* at the Musikverein; *ticket hotline: 505 81 90* Advent: various *Advent* and *Christmas markets*

December

First three weeks: *Mozart Festival* at the Konzerthaus; *ticket hotline: 24 20 02* Last day of the month: The *New Year's Trail* through the city centre lined with stalls, sideshows, music stages and dance tents. Highpoint is the ringing of the Pummerin Bell of St. Stephen's Cathedral

There's also a chance to twirl in three-four time

Palaces, churches, parks and monuments

Schönbrunn and St. Stephen's Cathedral, Ringstrasse and Belvedere – the former imperial city has some unique sights to offer

Visitors have no problems finding their way around Vienna. The medieval centre forms the heart of the city: officially the 1st district. Towering over it is Vienna's No. 1 landmark, St. Stephen's Cathedral, and numerous other Romanesque and Gothic churches bear witness to the deeply Catholic roots of the old imperial city. Here, too, is the Hofburg, the Imperial Palace, a huge complex from where, for a time, the Habsburgs ruled half of Europe. Remains of the Roman army camp *Vindobona* can be found scattered across the city centre. The majority of government ministries and key municipal and state economic and political power bases are congregated here. Most of the remaining historical monuments are situated along Ringstrasse, Vienna's showcase boulevard, which was laid out on the site of the original city ramparts.

An ideal place to relax: the Stadtpark laid out in English landscape style

Schloss Schönbrunn

Any sightseeing tour should begin in this historical 2-sq-km city centre. Ideally, you should go on foot, as the streets are largely traffic-free. Though not exactly cheap, a ride in a fiacre, one of Vienna's famous horse-drawn carriages, is a good way to soak up the atmosphere. The magnificent architecture of Ringstrasse can also be viewed from the comfort of the No. 1 or No. 2 trams.

Towards the periphery, the sights are more widely scattered. Until the *Anschluss*, the annexation of Austria by Nazi Germany in 1938, the 2nd district – beyond the Danube Canal and including the Prater recreational area – was home to Vienna's Jewish population. The

The Pestsäule, Baroque reminder of a deadly epidemic

3rd district includes the diplomatic quarter and the 8th district, close to the city centre, is considered the domain of the upper classes.

These former suburbs are ringed by the so-called 'Gürtel' or belt, a six-lane arterial road, which is currently being given a face-lift. Attractive architecture and landscapes beckon from the periphery – on the slopes of the Vienna Woods and along the Danube.

To make orientation in the city easier for visitors and give them an understanding of the city's history, the district administration has mounted white plaques decorated with the red and white national flag on 200 artistically and historically significant buildings, giving important background information.

FOUNTAINS & MONUMENTS

Donnerbrunnen [111 D4]

Vienna's most beautiful fountain, created in 1737–39, is a masterpiece of the great Baroque sculptor Georg Raphael Donner. The statue in the centre represents Providence, the peripheral figures personify Traun, Enns, Ybbs and March, the four main tributaries of the Danube on Austrian soil. Donner's lead sculptures were replaced in the 19th century with bronze replicas. The originals are in the Baroque Museum at the Lower Belvedere. *Neuer Markt; bus 3 A; U 1, U 3, Stephansplatz*

Mahnmal gegen Krieg und Faschismus [110 C4–5]

Erected in the late 1980s, a monument by Alfred Hrdlicka on the square behind the State Opera commemorates the victims of World War II and the Nazi dictatorship in Austria (1938–45). The group of sculptures includes the two-part, granite *Gates of Violence*, the bronze figure of the *Kneeling Jew* and the marble statue *Orpheus enters the Underworld*. A quotation from the declaration of independence of the Second Republic of 27 April 1945 is engraved on a stone column. *Albertinaplatz / Augustinerstrasse; bus: 3 A; U 1, U 2, U 4, Karlsplatz*

Maria-Theresien-Denkmal [110 B4–5]

The huge monument between the Museum of Fine Arts and the Museum of Natural History is by Caspar Zumbusch (1874–88) and shows the Empress amongst her most important comrades-in-arms in the service of the Austrian nation: army commanders Laudon, Daun, Khevenhüller and Traun on horseback, her advisors Kaunitz, Haugwitz, Liechtenstein and van Swieten standing. *Maria-Theresien-Platz; tram: D, J, 1, 2; bus: 57 A; U 2, Babenbergerstrasse; U 3, Volkstheater*

Pestsäule [111 D3]

The column dedicated to the Holy Trinity, donated by Emperor Leopold I, commemorates the devastating plague epidemic which carried off over 100,000 Viennese in 1679. The monumental high Baroque cloud formation was created by Lodovico Burnacini. The plinth is by Johann Bernhard Fischer von Erlach, the sculptures by Paul Strudel. *Graben; bus: 2 A, 3 A; U 1, U 3, Stephansplatz*

CEMETERIES & TOMBS

Kaisergruft [111 D4]

★ Since 1632, all Habsburg rulers and their closest relatives have found their final resting place here, under the Capuchin Church. Their hearts, however, lie separately in the Augustine Church and their remaining internal organs in the catacombs of St. Stephen's Cathedral. The last Emperor to be buried here was Franz Joseph I in 1916. The final burial took place with much ceremony as late as

MARCO POLO Highlights »Sightseeing«

★ **Stephansdom**
Vienna's Gothic landmark (page 33)

★ **Schloss Schönbrunn**
The Habsburg Versailles (page 27)

★ **Ringstraße**
Parade of *Gründerzeit* monuments on Vienna's star boulevard (page 38)

★ **Belvedere**
Prince Eugene's Baroque dream palace (page 22)

★ **Hofburg**
Heart of the empire – with Lipizzaner, choir boys, treasure chamber and the National Library (page 24)

★ **Kaisergruft**
Last resting place of the Habsburgs (page 21)

★ **Hundertwasserhaus**
Many-coloured architectural spectacle (page 25)

★ **Karl-Marx-Hof**
Monumental symbol of the 'red Vienna' of the 1920s (page 25)

★ **Grinzing**
Heuriger – a cosy get-to-gether under the chestnut trees (page 36)

★ **Prater**
Green oasis of fun and sport, with 'Wurstelprater' and giant ferris wheel (page 35)

1989, when the widow of Charles I, Empress Zita, was laid to rest. Of the 138 metal coffins, the richly decorated double sarcophagus designed by Balthasar Ferdinand Moll for Maria Theresia and her husband Franz I Stephan of Lorraine is the finest. *Daily 9.30 am to 4 pm; Neuer Markt; bus: 3 A; U 1, U 3, Stephansplatz*

Sankt Marx [124–125 C–D5]

Vienna's only remaining – and consequently protected – Biedermeier cemetery is a haven for the melancholic, despite being buffeted by urban highways. A walk through the park-like memorial garden with its roughly 6,000 ivy-clad gravestones is like a journey back to the early 19th century. The most famous permanent guest is Wolfgang Amadeus Mozart. His life is commemorated by a monument (No. 179). Even today, however, no one knows for certain where his body was actually buried on 6 December 1791. *June–Aug: daily 7 am–7 pm; May&Sept: 7 am–6 pm; Oct&Apr: 7 am–5 pm; Nov–Mar: 7 am until dusk; Leberstrasse 6–8; tram: 71*

Zentralfriedhof [127 E4]

Since its opening in 1874, over 3 million people have been laid to rest in this 2.4 sq km cemetery. In terms of cultural history, the graves of honour are the most significant feature. These include those of Beethoven, Schubert and both Strausses, dramatist Johann Nestroy, writer Franz Werfel and actor and satirist Helmut Qualtinger – just a few of the many intellectual greats who are buried here. In the extensive and atmospheric Israelite section lie, among others dramatist

and novelist Arthur Schnitzler and poet and satirist Karl Kraus. The huge Dr.-Karl-Lueger-Memorial Church, a powerful work by Secessionist Max Hegele (built in 1907 to 1910), is worth a look. A plan of the cemetery is available at the main entrance. *Nov–Feb: 8 am to 5 pm; Mar, Apr, Sept&Oct: 7 am to 6 pm; May–Aug: 7 am–7 pm; Simmeringer Hauptstrasse 232–244; tram: 71*

HOUSES & PALACES

Akademie der Wissenschaften [111 E3]

This palatial building, resembling in style French Classicism, is by Jadot de Ville-Issey, imperial building inspector to Maria Theresia. Built in 1753–55, it served originally as the Great Hall of the Old University. Since the end of the 19th century, it has been the seat of the Academy of Science. The banqueting hall, richly decorated with stucco work and ceiling frescos, is particularly interesting. *Dr.-Ignaz-Seipel-Platz 2; tram: 1, 2; bus: 2 A; U 3, Stubentor*

Belvedere [124 A2–3]

★ A must for every visitor is the former summer palace of Prince Eugene. The sprawling complex, consisting of two palaces, is held not only to be Johann Lukas von Hildebrandt's masterpiece, but is also one of the most superb Baroque creations ever. Situated on a hill, with Vienna, as it were, at its feet, the ◄◊► Obere (upper) Belvedere (1721–23) was built by the legendary army commander from Savoy and conqueror of the Turks merely for representative purposes. The preciously furnished rooms of this long, brilliantly structured building house the Österreichische Gallerie (Austrian Gallery). The 'noble knight' himself actually lived in the Untere (lower) Belvedere (1714 to 1716), a scarcely less grand structure with a sumptuous Marble Hall with frescos and stucco work, a Mirrored Hall and a magnificent Gallery. Today, it houses the Barockmuseum (Baroque Museum). In the neighbouring Orangerie is the Museum mittelalterlicher Kunst (Museum of Medieval Art). A more than 500-m-long terraced garden divides both palaces. It has been restored to its original Baroque form, including rose beds, hedges and water courses. *Garden: daily 6.30 am to 6 pm; summer: until 9 pm; museums: Tues–Sun 10 am–5 pm or 6 pm, Thurs until 9 pm; upper entrance: Prinz-Eugen-Strasse 27; lower entrance: Rennweg 6A; tram: 71*

Bundeskanzleramt [110 B3]

The former secret Imperial Chancellery (1717–20, Johann Lukas von Hildebrandt) has been the seat of Austrian power for over 250 years. Maria Theresia's chancellor Prince Kaunitz performed his duties here, as did Prince Metternich, until the revolution of 1848. The Congress of Vienna convened here in 1814–15. Today, the Baroque building contains the offices of the Federal Chancellor and Foreign Minister; those of the Austrian President are situated opposite. *Ballhausplatz 2; bus: 2 A; U 3, Herrengasse*

Burgtheater [110 B3]

This holy shrine of German-language theatre is not only interesting for what happens on stage. The building itself, built to plans by Gottfried Semper and Karl von Hasenauer in 1874–88, deserves closer inspection: the façade in the style of the Italian high Renaissance, with its colossal busts of great men of letters above the windows, the magnificent interior with its staircases and interval

Equine Ballet

Watch the legendary Lipizzaner being put through their paces

A peculiarity of Vienna is the presence of stables right in the middle of the city, in the imperial palace to be exact: the Spanish Riding School with its famous white Lipizzaner horses. Spectators can watch the willing pupils during morning training (10 am–noon; ask for dates at your hotel or Tourist Information Offices); *tickets: Visitor Centre, Michaelerplatz 1; (Tues–Sat 9 am to 5.30 pm; 11 Euro)*. Alternatively, visit a gala performance *(11 am and 6 pm)*. Tickets can be applied for in writing from the *Spanish Riding School, Hofburg; 1010 Vienna, Michaelerplatz 1; Fax 01-535 01 86; www.spanische-reitschule.com;* or bought from advance booking offices and travel agents.

rooms adorned with frescos and the 1,500-seat auditorium. *Dr.-Karl-Lueger-Ring 2; guided tours (approx. 1 hr): daily 3 pm, Sun, publ. hols also 11 am, otherwise by appointment (Tel. 514 44-41 40); tram: D, 1, 2*

Haus der Musik [111 D5]

On seven floors of this lavishly restored palace you can take a multimedia interactive journey through the world of sound. Anything from the Vienna Philharmonic Orchestra, founded in 1842, to the Future Music Blender and from the origins of sound to Vienna's star composers and hyperinstruments for do-it-yourself experiments. *Daily 10 am to 10 pm; Seilerstätte 30; tram: D, J, 1, 2, 71; U 1, U 2, U 4, Karlsplatz*

Hofburg [110 B–C 3–4]

★ For over 600 years, from the granting of Austrian lands to the Habsburg Rudolf I (1276) until the abdication of Emperor Charles (1918), 'the castle' was the seat of the Austrian dynasty. Originally comparatively small, it grew down the centuries in proportion to the power wielded and empire ruled by its residents to become the intricate complex of 18 wings and 19 courtyards of today. The oldest part is the Schweizerhof (Swiss Courtyard), from where you enter the Schatzkammer (Treasure Chamber) and the Gothic Burgkapelle (Palace Chapel). Additions made in the 16th century include the Stallburg (Stables), the Amalientrakt (Amalia Residence) and the red, black and gold Schweizertor (Swiss Gate), the entrance to the Swiss Courtyard. The Leopoldinische Trakt (Leopoldine Wing) was added in the 17th century and in the 18th, under the guidance of Johann Lukas von Hildebrandt and Joseph Emanuel Fischer von Erlach, the Reichskanzleitrakt (Imperial Chancellery Wing). He and his son also built the Winterreitschule (Winter Riding School), in which the Lipizzaner practise their art, plus the Nationalbibliothek (Austrian National Library), a major example of Austrian Baroque, whose Grand Hall with its huge cupola, has often earned the title most beautiful reading room in the world. The Michaelertrakt (St. Michael Wing) was completed at the end of the 19th century. Finally, between 1891–1913, the Neue Burg (New Palace) marked what was to be the beginning of a much larger project – an Imperial Forum – whose realisation was prevented by the outbreak of World War I.

Of the total of 2,500 rooms in this stone labyrinth, only a small number are open to view. These

Fiacre in front of the Hofburg

include the Imperial Apartments and the Silver Collection which are both reached from the domed hall of the St. Michael Wing. Also open are the Treasure Chamber, the Palace Chapel, the Great Hall of the National Library, the Spanische Hofreitschule (Spanish Riding School) and finally, in the New Palace, the Collection of Arms and Armour, the Collection of Ancient Musical Instruments and the Ephesus Museum, all part of the Kunsthistorisches Museum (Museum of Fine Arts). In addition, the Hofburg houses the offices of the Federal Chancellor, a much-used congress centre, various public offices, private and official apartments and some shops in the pedestrian precinct between the Burghof and Heldenplatz. *Michaelerplatz, Josefsplatz, Heldenplatz, Ballhausplatz. National Library; Josefsplatz 1; mid-May–Oct: daily 10 am–4 pm, Thurs until 7 pm; Nov–mid-May: Mon to Sat 10 am–2 pm; tram: D, J, 1, 2; bus: 2 A, 3 A; U 1, U 2, U 4, Karlsplatz, U 3, Herrengasse*

Hundertwasserhaus [118 B–C5]

★ This rather unusual municipal residential block is the work of painter Friedensreich Hundertwasser, who discarded all rules governing symmetry and right-angles to create a much marvelled-at work of art – with special authorisation from the planning department! Trees and bushes grow on roofs and balconies. The walls and floors are curved in many places and the façades are colourfully painted. The building can generally only be viewed from the outside, out of consideration for the residents of the 50 apartments. *(Löwengasse/*

Bizarre. the Hundertwasserhaus, built in 1985

Kegelgasse; tram: N). Hundertwasser's *Toilet of Modern Art* is, however, accessible to all visitors, in the shopping centre at *Kalke Village, Kegelgasse 37–39.*

Karl-Marx-Hof [113 D–E 1–2]

★ The prime example of innovative council housing, by which Vienna's Social Democrat municipal council was able to ease substantially the desolate housing situation of the working classes in the 1920s. Built in 1927–30 to plans by Karl Ehn, the block is 1,200 m long and contains 1,600 apartments. It was painstakingly renovated some time ago. *Heiligenstädter Strasse 82 to 92/12.-Februar-Platz; tram: D; bus: 10 A, 11 A, 39 A; U 4, Heiligenstadt*

Kunsthistorisches und Naturhistorisches Museum [110 A3–4]

The two museums, standing opposite each other and almost identical from the outside, were created by the architects of the Ringstrasse, Gottfried Semper and Karl von Hasenauer. Inside, the monumental buildings are decorated with wall and ceiling pictures by Ernst and Gustav Klimt, Michael Munkáczy, Hans Makart and others. *Maria-Theresien-Platz; tram: D, J, 1, 2; bus: 57 A; U 2, Babenbergerstrasse, U 3, Volkstheater*

Looshaus [110 C3]

Scarcely another building in Vienna has caused so much controversy as this residential and commercial building, completed in 1911. Dubbed 'the house without eyebrows' because of the absence of ledges or pediments above the windows, it was derided due to its bare exterior and its creator, Adolf Loos, was harshly criticised for his tastelessness. This daring work, whose elegant but restrained façade of green marble and glass contrasts markedly with the neo-Baroque Hofburg opposite, was in fact a milestone on the path towards the functional building style of the 20th century. *Michaelerplatz 3; bus: 2 A, 3 A; U 3, Herrengasse*

Majolikahaus [122 C2]

A feast for the eyes for all lovers of Art Nouveau: Otto Wagner's apartment block with its façade of colourful intertwining plants and flowers painted on weather-resistant majolica ceramic tiles. Wagner was also responsible for the filigree gold ornamentation of the corner house next door, to the right. The medallions depicting women's heads are by Kolo Moser, co-founder of the Secessionist movement and the artists' co-operative, the 'Wiener Werkstätten'. *Linke Wienzeile 38 and 40; U 4, Kettenbrückengasse*

Neidhart-Fresken [110 C3]

In 1979 these Gothic frescoes were discovered unexpectedly during rebuilding of an apartment. Dating back to around 1400, they illustrate scenes from the songs of minnesinger Neidhart von Reuental. *Tuchlauben 19; Tues–Sun 9 am to noon; bus: 2 A, 3 A; U 1, U 3, Stephansplatz*

Neues Rathaus [110 A2–3]

The neo-Gothic New City Hall was built in 1872–83. It is the seat of the mayor and municipal and regional government. The interior – the colonnaded courtyard, the magnificent staircases and huge banqueting hall – can be viewed as part of a guided tour. On top of the almost 100-m-high tower stands a 6-m-high figure of the 'Rathausmann', a sort of iron mascot looking out over the city. In summer, opera and concert films are shown on a giant screen in front of the main façade's filigree loggias, balconies and pointed arched windows. The Rathauspark in front is decorated with numerous monuments. *Friedrich-Schmidt-Platz 1; free guided tours: Mon, Wed&Fri 1 pm (except for publ. holidays and when in session, Tel. 525 50); tram: 1, 2; U 2, Rathaus*

Palais Ferstel [110 C2–3]

This magnificent, Venetian-style example of Vienna's Ringstrasse architecture was built in 1856–60 by Heinrich von Ferstel for the National Bank. Until 1877, it also housed the Stock Exchange. The Café Central on the corner of Herrengasse and Strauchgasse was famed as a meeting place of men of letters. After decades of neglect, the huge complex, which is accessible from three sides and includes an exclusive glass-roofed shopping arcade, was renovated at great expense in the early 1980s. *Freyung 2/Herrengasse 17; bus: 1 A, 2 A; U 3, Herrengasse*

Parlament [110 A3–4]

Built in 1873–83, the Parliament building is the seat of both the National Council and the Federal Council. By echoing the style of classical antiquity and placing a fountain with a figure of goddess of wisdom Pallas Athene in front of the main entrance, the architect, Theophil Hansen, sought to call to mind the Greek democratic ideals. *Dr.-Karl-Renner Ring 3; guided tours (except when in session): Mon to Thurs 11 am, 3 pm, Fri 11 am, 1 pm, 2 pm, 3 pm; July–mid-Sept: Mon–Fri also 9 am, 10 am, 1 pm, 2 pm, Sat&Sun by prior arrangement only (Tel. 401 10-25 70); tram: D, J, 1, 2, 49*

Postsparkasse [111 F3]

A trailblazer in terms of modern architecture, the coolly elegant Post Office Savings Bank building is the masterpiece of great innovator Otto Wagner. The architect always preached the indivisibility of practicality and beauty, and his buildings have shaped the face of Vienna. Not only the façade is worth a closer look – clad in marble and granite slabs and crowned by two aluminium guardian angels – but also the glass-roofed hall with its painstakingly planned furnishings – also by Wagner. *Georg-Coch-Platz 2; tram: 1, 2, N*

Schloss Schönbrunn [120 A–C 4–6]

★ The Habsburg's summer residence, also known as Austria's Versailles, is Vienna's top attraction, along with St. Stephen's Cathedral and the Belvedere. Palace and grounds, though magnificent are in no way showy or pompous, but seem rather charming and graceful. The palace harks back to a bourgeois manor house which Emperor Maximilian II bought in 1559 and had converted into a hunting lodge. Destroyed by the invading Turks in 1683, the palace was re-built to plans by Johann Bernhard Fischer von Erlach in much the same form as we see it today, with two side wings, the broad Courtyard of Honour facing the road and the staircase on the garden side.

Schönbrunn only became the glorious focal point of the monarchy under Empress Maria Theresia, who lived here with her consort Franz I Stephan of Lorraine and their 16 children. At her bidding, the young architect Nicolaus Pacassi re-designed the palace in the years 1744–49 according to the then, late-Baroque style, adding another storey and numerous additional balconies and staircases, the charming Baroque Schlosstheater (Palace Theatre) and opening a passage through the central section. The private and representational apartments were decorated in the new, elegant and dainty Rococo style.

Puppet theatre at Schönbrunn

In the 19th and early 20th centuries, Schönbrunn saw history in the making. Twice, in 1805 and 1809, Napoleon took up quarters here. In 1814–15 the delegates at the Congress of Vienna danced in its palatial rooms. In 1832 Napoleon's son from his marriage to the Archduchess Marie Louise of Austria, the Duke of Reichstadt, died within its walls. Shortly before, in 1830, Franz Joseph was born, who as Emperor welcomed kings, sultans and tsars to his beloved Schönbrunn. Finally, in 1918, two years after the death of the long-serving Emperor, his great nephew Charles signed his declaration of abdication in the Blue Salon.

Of the over 1,400 rooms, some 50 of the most beautiful can be visited as part of various guided tours, including the Great Gallery,

the Vieux Laque Room, the 'Millions Room', whose rosewood panelling is decorated with 260 inlaid Persian and Indian miniatures, the Napoleon Room with its huge Brussels tapestries, the Round Chinese Cabinet, where Maria Theresia held her private conferences and Emperor Franz Joseph's spartanly furnished study and salon. Also of interest is the unique collection of 60 state carriages in the Imperial Coach Collection, to the west of the Courtyard of Honour, plus special children's activities in the main wing. Be sure to take an extended tour of the delightful park. In addition to the flower beds, hedges, rose gardens and avenues which are lovingly and painstakingly cared for, it features many fountains and monuments, a huge Palm House, a maze and Vienna's zoo. This architectural gem from the Baroque era was founded in 1752, making it the oldest animal collection in the world, and now boasts a new 'Desert Experience House'.

The ◁▷ Gloriette, which crowns a hill in the park, commemorates the victory over the Prussians near Kolin in 1757. The graceful, newly glazed building, which corresponds to the original, now houses a café.

What better way to round off your tour of Schönbrunn than by listening to a concert in the Orangery or an opera at the *Marionettentheater* (Puppet Theatre) or in the Schlosstheater (Palace Theatre)? The latter also stages occasional operettas and drama.

Inside Tip

Main entrance: Schönbrunner Schlossstrasse; tram: 10, 58; access also via Hietzinger Tor, Hietzinger Hauptstrasse: U 4, Hietzing; Meid-

linger Tor, Grünbergstrasse: U 4, Schönbrunn; Hohenbergstrasse entrance: bus: 8 A, 63 A; palace gardens open all year round, daily 6.30 am until dusk; apartments (guided tours only): Apr, June, Sept&Oct: 8.30 am–5 pm; July &Aug: until 7 pm; Nov–Mar: until 4.30 pm; children's tours: Sat&Sun and publ. hols: 10.30 am, 2.30 pm; 'Children's Experience': Fri&Sat 1 pm–5 pm, Sun and publ. hols 10 am–5 pm; Imperial Coach Collection: Apr–Oct: daily 9 am–6 pm; Nov–Mar: Tues–Sun 10 am–4 pm; zoo: Nov–Jan: daily 9 am–4.30 pm; Feb: 9 am–5 pm; Mar&Oct: 9 am to 5.30 pm; Apr: 9 am–6 pm; May to Sept: 9 am–6.30 pm; maze: Apr to June, Sept: daily 9 am–5.30 pm; July&Aug: until 7 pm; Oct: until 5 pm; Nov: until 4 pm; Palm House: May–Sept: daily 9.30 am–5.30 pm; Oct–Apr: 9.30 am–4.30 pm; Gloriette/roof access: Apr–Oct: daily 8 am–5 pm; café open all year round, daily 9 am until dusk; concerts in the Orangery all year round: Tel. 812 50 04; Puppet Theatre all year round: Tel. 817 32 47

Secession [110 C6]

In 1897–98 Josef Maria Olbrich conceived this exhibition and meeting place for the 'Wiener Secession', a group of avant-garde artists who had previously split away from their more conservative colleagues in the 'Künstlerhaus' artists' association. Once mockingly nicknamed 'cabbage head', the building, adorned by an intricate crown of golden leaves, is held to be a

3,000 leaves intertwine to make the gold cupola of the Secession building

masterpiece of Vienna Art Nouveau. Gustav Klimt's Beethoven frieze can be seen in the basement. *Friedrichstrasse 12; Tues, Wed, Fri–Sun and publ. hols. 10 am to 6 pm, Thurs 10 am–8 pm; U 1, U 2, U 4, Karlsplatz*

Staatsoper [110 C5]
The inauguration in 1869 of the Imperial and Royal Court Opera Theatre – with its loggia, side arcades and metal barrel roof – was greeted with such vehement criticism that one of its architects, Eduard van der Nüll, committed suicide and the other, August von Siccardsburg, died of a heart attack shortly afterwards! In the meantime, the Romantic-Historicist building, which was badly damaged during the final weeks of World War II, has found a place in Viennese hearts as a symbol of their musical culture. The interior boasts a fresco-lined staircase, the Schwind Foyer, the Gobelin Room (now Gustav-Mahler Room) and Marble Room and an auditorium seating 2,200. These feature as part of various guided tours. *(Notice of times is given at the side entrance or under Tel. 514 44-26 13). Opernring 2; tram: D, J, 1, 2; bus: 59 A; U 1, U 2, U 4, Karlsplatz*

CHURCHES

Augustinerkirche [110 C4]
Built in the 1430s, the Church of the Augustinian Friars, a Gothic hall church with beautiful fan- and ribbed vault ceilings, served the Habsburgs as court parish church from the mid-17th century onwards. Children born into the imperial family were christened here, many family members, including Emperor Franz Joseph and Sisi, took their marriage vows at its altar. Of particular interest in the narrow, tall three-nave interior are the marble memorial to Archduchess Maria Christine by Classicist sculptor Antonio Canova, the Gothic St. George's Chapel and

Take it Easy!

Get back to nature – it's never far away

There comes a time when everyone yearns to leave the city for the countryside. In Vienna the way out of the maze of streets into the surrounding green is remarkably short.
The meadows and footpaths of the Vienna Woods or the largely untouched flood meadows along the Danube can be reached from anywhere in the city within half an hour, thanks to a comprehensive network of underground railway, bus and tram routes. Particularly pretty and very close at hand is the *Alte Donau*. Ten minutes by U-Bahn (U 1) from St. Stephen's Cathedral, this branch of the Danube was separated from the main river some 130 years ago and now boasts delightfully old-fashioned amusements and cosy tourist cafés.

finally the so-called 'Herzgrüfterl', the crypt in which 54 urns are kept, containing the hearts of the Habsburgs. *Tours of the crypt by prior arrangement only: Tel. 533 70 99; Augustinerstrasse 3; tram: D, J, 1, 2; U 1, U 2, U 4, Karlsplatz*

Dominikanerkirche   [111 E3]

The façade of the mid 17th century Baroque Dominican Church, with its staircase, gables and pilasters, harks back to Roman times, yet the freshly renovated interior overwhelms the visitor with the full glory of Viennese early Baroque. The most arresting feature is the altarpiece of the high altar by Romantic artist Leopold Kupelwieser in 1839. *Postgasse 4; tram: 1, 2; bus: 2 A; U 3, Stubentor*

Jesuitenkirche   [111 E3]

Insider Tip

What fascinates the visitor above all about the Jesuit Church are the illusionist ceiling paintings, which suggest a central cupola above the nave. Built at the beginning of the 17th century, the church (also known as the University Church) was re-designed along high Baroque lines by Andrea Pozzo scarcely a century later. The twin-tower façade graces one of the most idyllic city centre squares. *Dr.-Ignaz-Seipel-Platz; tram: 1, 2; bus: 2 A; U 3, Stubentor*

Karlskirche   [111 D6]

When, in 1713, a plague epidemic killed over 8,000 Viennese, Emperor Charles VI promised to build a church in honour of Saint Borromeo, should the horror come to a rapid end. The votive Church of St. Charles Borromeo is a grandiose creation by Johann Bernhard Fischer

The façade of the Karlskirche: Fischer von Erlach's masterpiece

von Erlach and his son Joseph Emanuel and was consecrated in 1737. It is held to be one of the major works of European Baroque. With its huge cupola, coated in green patina, and the two equally imposing triumphal columns flanking the centre section of the Greek-inspired façade, the church serves not only to glorify God, but also to underline the claim to imperial power of the Habsburgs, who had shortly before defeated the Turks in battle. The oval-shaped interior, painted in subtle pastel shades, culminates in a monumental cupola fresco by Johann Michael Rottmayr. Thanks to the ongoing renovation work, this can be inspected at close quarters from a scaffolding lift. *Mon–Sat 9.30 am–12.30 pm, 1 pm*

to 6 pm, Sun 1 pm–6 pm; Karlsplatz; tram: D; U 1, U 2; U 4, Karlsplatz

Kirche am Hof [110 C2–3]

The first Jesuit church in Vienna –
the Church of the Nine Choirs of
Angels, to give it its full name – was
originally Gothic, then re-built
following a fire at the beginning of
the 17th century in the Baroque
style. Today's unusual façade was
created in 1662 by Carlo Antonio
Carlone. It was from the balcony of
this church in 1806 that Emperor
Franz II, bowing to pressure from
Napoleon, announced his renunci-
ation of the crown, thereby bringing the curtain down on the Holy
Roman Empire. *Am Hof; bus: 1 A;
U 3, Herrengasse*

Kirche am Steinhof [126 C3]

Otto Wagner built this major
example of Viennese Art Nouveau
between 1904 and 1907 in the
grounds of the 'Am Steinhof'
psychiatric hospital on the slopes of
the Vienna Woods. Thanks to its
brilliant white façade, flanked by
two small towers, and its copper
dome, the cube-shaped Steinhof
Church can be seen for miles
around. *Guided tours: Sat 2.30 pm
to 4 pm; groups by prior arrangement only; Tel. 910 60-112 04;
Baumgartner Höhe 1; bus: 47 A,
48 A*

Kirche zur Heiligsten
Dreifaltigkeit [126 C4]

Built in the 1970s to plans by great
sculptor Fritz Wotruba, the inter-
locking concrete cubes and glass
walls of the Church of the Most
Holy Trinity give it the appearance
of a giant sculpture, way out in the

open countryside. *Sat 2 pm–8 pm,
Sun and publ. hols. 9 am–5 pm;
guided tours by arrangement only
(Tel. 888 50 03); Mauer, Georgs-
gasse/Rysergasse; bus: 60 A*

Maria am Gestade [111 D2]

The main attraction at this narrow,
Gothic Church of Our Lady on the
Steps (1343–1414), which once
stood directly on the steep banks of
an old branch of the Danube, is the
delicate, seven-sided dome-shaped
helm roof. In terms of its structure,
the church is notable for the slight
bend in the axis between nave and
choir. A shrine before the altar of a
side chapel contains the relics of St.
Clemens Maria Hofbauer, patron
saint of Vienna. *Salvatorgasse/Pas-
sauer Platz; bus: 1 A, 3 A*

Michaelerkirche [110 C3]

Behind the Classicist façade and
crowned by an octagonal tower, the
venerable St. Michael's Church
dates back largely to the late
Romanesque period (early 13th
century). The choir is Gothic, the
Baroque portico is decorated with
statues. *Michaelerplatz; bus: 2 A;
U 3, Herrengasse*

Minoritenkirche [110 B3]

The three-nave hall church – its
roof turret typical of mendicant
orders – is a product of the Gothic
period (14th century). Later
Baroque modifications to the
Minorite Church disappeared in the
course of a re-orientation towards
the Gothic style at the end of the
18th century. The lavish tracery of
the windows and the splendid
portal (1350) are truly magnificent
features. *Minoritenplatz; U 3, Herrengasse*

Peterskirche [111 D3]

St. Peter's Church was built in the first half of the 18th century to plans by Gabriel Montani and Johann Lukas von Hildebrandt. It rates as one of the most outstanding works of Austrian Baroque. Dazzling focal point of the interior is the cupola fresco by Johann M. Rottmayr celebrating the Assumption of Mary. *Petersplatz; bus: 2 A, 3 A*

Piaristenkirche [116 B4]

The twin-tower parish and monastery church of the Piarist Order, Maria Treu, is based on designs by Johann Lukas von Hildebrandt. Its ceiling is decorated with wonderfully delicate frescoes by Franz Anton Maulpertsch. In summer, the idyllic square in front of the church with its Heuriger is a popular place to sit outside. *Jodok-Fink-Platz, tram: J; bus: 13 A*

Ruprechtskirche [111 D2]

Vienna's oldest existing church was founded, legend has it, in around 740. Its nave and the lower tower storeys date back to the Romanesque period in the early 12th century. *Ruprechtsplatz; bus: 2 A; U 1, U 4, Schwedenplatz*

Stephansdom [111 D3]

★ Lovingly nicknamed 'Steffl' by the Viennese, the city's landmark, St. Stephen's Cathedral, is the most significant Gothic structure in Austria. The history of its construction reaches back as far as 1147 and the consecration of a Romanesque church. This was replaced in the mid-13th century by a new church in the same style, the remains of which – the giant main doorway

with the two Heathe[n] still form the western [...]

Today's building gr[...] between 1303 and 1340, the three-nave Albertine Choir; from 1359, at the bidding of its donator Habsburg Duke Rudolf IV, the nave with its magnificent star- and fan-vaulted ceiling and the 137-m-high South Tower. Its planned counterpart, the North Tower, was never completed and was topped with a Renaissance-style helm roof in 1579. Under this hangs the 'Pummerin', the 21-tonne cathedral bell, the largest in the country. It was cast following the second Turkish siege of Vienna (1683) using the bronze from captured enemy cannon.

The interior, dubbed 'the most solemn in the world' by Adolf Loos, contains many unique art treasures. The most important are the pulpit by Anton Pilgram (1514/15), the Gothic Viennese Neustädter Altar (1447), the tomb of Emperor Frederick III, which Niclas Gerhaert van Leyden took over forty years to complete (1467–1513) and the monument to Prince Eugene of Savoy (1754). Take a look down in the catacombs at the tombs of 15 early Habsburgs and urns containing the internal organs of the other 56 members of the dynasty whose remains are buried in the Kaisergruft.

Those who climb the 343 narrow steps up to the ◀ℐ▶ Türmerstube (the former watchman's lookout) in the South Tower are rewarded with fantastic views of the city.

Guided tours of the cathedral: Mon–Sat 10.30 am, 3 pm, Sun and publ. hols. 3 pm only; evening tours with tour of roof: June–Sept: Sat

7 pm; catacombs (guided tour only): Mon–Sat 10 am–11.30 am, 1.30 pm–4 pm, Sun and publ. hols. every 30 mins in the afternoon; South Tower stairs: daily 9 am to 5.30 pm; lift to 'Pummerin' in North Tower: Apr, June, Sept&Oct: daily 9 am–5.30 pm; July&Aug: 8 am–6 pm; Nov–Mar: 8.30 am to 5 pm; Stephansplatz; U 1, U 3, Stephansplatz

Votivkirche   [110 A–B1]
When the young Emperor Franz Joseph I survived an assassination attempt in 1853, his brother, Archduke Ferdinand Max, initiated the building of an atonement church. A huge, twin-tower church ensued to plans by Heinrich von Ferstel in the style of French Gothic cathedrals. Consecrated in 1879, it represents one of the major examples of severe

Historicism. *Rooseveltplatz; tram: D, 1, 2, 37, 38, 40–44; U 2, Schottentor*

PARKS, GARDENS, RECREATIONAL AREAS

Burggarten   [110 C4–5]
Laid out in 1818 exclusively for the imperial family, the garden was only opened to the public some 100 years later. The well-kept grounds feature memorials to Mozart and the two Emperors Franz I Stephan of Lorraine and Franz Joseph I. New to the garden and well worth a visit: the Butterfly House in the Wintergarten, including a restaurant. *Apr–Oct: Mon–Fri 10 am to 4.45 pm, Sat&Sun and publ. hols. 10 am–6.15 pm; winter: daily 10 am–3.45 pm; Burgring/Opernring; tram: D, J, 1, 2; bus: 57 A*

Inside Tip

Between the Covers

Enough reading matter about Vienna to fill a library

To get you in the mood, try the classic thriller *The Third Man* in which Graham Greene grippingly portrays the grey, cliché-ridden post-1945 Vienna and transports you to the depths of the city's sewers. Veza Canetti describes Jewish Vienna in *Yellow Street*. Of the highest literary quality is Robert Musil's *The Man Without Qualities*, characterising the typical Viennese way of life and thought around the time of World War I. *Wittgenstein's Vienna* by Allan Janik and Stephen Toulmin takes a look at the city and the fall of the Austro-Hungarian Empire through the eyes of one of its most prominent philosophers. *Vienna: Art and Architecture* by Rolf Toman is a classic on the subject. Peter Csendes' Historical Dictionary of Vienna is good to dip into. Music lovers should try *Beethoven and the Construction of Genius: Musical Politics in Vienna 1792-1803* by Tia DeNora. Another name which is inseparable from that of Vienna is Sigmund Freud. Peter Gay has written a definitive biography, *Freud a Life for Our Time*.

Neue Donau [114 A–C 1–6]

The 200-m-wide and some 20-km-long artificial island between the Danube and the relief canal was created in the 1970s and 1980s as part of large-scale flood-protection projects. It was transformed into a huge recreational area with seemingly endless bathing beaches, cycle and footpaths, playgrounds and sports facilities, restaurants, ice-cream parlours and discotheques. Between the new and old Danube, a little to the west of UN City, the 252-m-high ⚡ *Donauturm* [115 D–E4] (Danube Tower) soars over the *Donaupark* (Danube Park). Tower and park were created in 1964 for the International Horticultural Show. From the revolving restaurant at the top, there is a panoramic view across the Danube, the city and right across to the Vienna Woods.

Prater [118–119 B–F 3–6]

★ This landscape of woods and meadows, criss-crossed by truncated branches of the Danube, extends for almost 15 km. It was adopted by the Viennese for recreational purposes as early as 1766, after Joseph II had made this once imperial hunting ground accessible to the public. To this day, the Prater constitutes one of the city's huge, green 'lungs'. Sports fans enjoy a wide range of facilities: an extensive network of cycle and footpaths, tennis courts, golf course, trotting course and flat-race course, cycling and football stadia.

In the westerly section, close to the city, a conglomeration of amusement stalls and inns grew up at the beginning of the 19th century – the so-called 'Wurstelprater'.

Riesenrad at the Prater

A trace of nostalgic flair can still be felt in today's funfair: in old-fashioned ghost trains and other amusement stalls, shooting galleries and shady beer gardens. In between all these, the usual array of entertainment venues, from flashing neon one-armed bandit and pinball machines to dizzying rides with high tech catapults, has taken hold.

A must for every visitor to the city is surely the ten-minute ride on the ⚡ *Riesenrad* [118 C3] (giant ferris wheel), a 67-m-high iron construction erected in 1896–97. A symbol of Vienna, it achieved world fame as the backdrop to Carol Reed's post-war thriller *The Third Man* with Orson Welles. From the red cabins there's a wonderful view of the Prater, the city centre and districts to the east *(daily, depending on season, from 9 am or 10 am to 8 pm, 10 pm or midnight; www.wienerriesenrad.com)*.

Not far from the ferris wheel is the departure point of the *Liliputbahn,* a 4-km-long miniature rail-

...ich is particularly popular with families. Next door, a *Planetarium* takes you on a trip up to the stars (*Tel. 729 54 94-0*). *Wurstelprater; tram: O, 5, 21; S-Bahn: 1, 3, 7, 15; U 1, Praterstern*

Stadtpark [111 E–F 4–5]
This quiet green oasis was opened in 1862 and was the first park to be laid out by the municipal authorities. Its winding paths are lined with monuments. The most famous of these depicts Johann Strauss junior striking up a waltz. Further tributes are to Schubert, Bruckner, Lehár, Robert Stolz, and others. A fine staircase and pavilions overlook the River Wien, close to the U-Bahn station Stadtpark – designed by Art-Nouveau architect Friedrich Ohmann. *Parkring; tram: 1, 2; U 4, Stadtpark, U 3, Stubentor*

Craft market in Spittelberg

Volksgarten [110 B3–4]
After Napoleon had the fortified castle razed to the ground in 1809, the free space was used to create a park 'for the people'. Peer Nobile, builder of the Outer Castle Gateway, placed his 'Temple of Theseus' in its centre to house Antonio Canova's marble sculpture of Theseus which now graces the staircase of the Kunsthistorisches Museum (Museum of Fine Arts). In two quiet corners there are memorials to Empress Elisabeth and Franz Grillparzer. The rose garden close to the Burgtheater exit is famous for its beautiful display. *Tram: D, 1, 2, J, 46, 49; bus: 2 A, 48 A*

URBAN DISTRICTS

Grinzing [112 A–C 1–2]
★ Vienna boasts many 'Heuriger' districts, from Mauer on the city's southern boundary to Stammersdorf on the other side of the Danube. The traditional wine taverns are famous for their typically Viennese, welcoming atmosphere and nowhere will you find so many, classic examples as in this wine-growing village on the northeastern slopes of the Vienna Woods. Admittedly, the majority of tourist groups also stop off here in search of the old clichés. *Grinzingerstrasse, Himmelstrasse, Sandgasse and Cobenzlgasse; tram: 38; bus: 38 A*

Spittelberg [110 A5] Inside Tip
The narrow, pedestrianised alleyways have a picturesque suburban feel, with galleries, boutiques, craft shops and cosy pubs. The quarter lies in the 7th district, directly

Top Fit!

Train first, then relax –
shape up to the city jungle

Relaxation for mind and body is guaranteed at the Oberlaa thermal spa, with whirlpools, sauna and solarium. Tone your muscles at the wellness park on a wide range of apparatus. *Thermalbad Oberlaa, Kurbadstrasse 14; Mon–Sat 8.45 am–10 pm, Sun 7.45 am–10 pm (last admission 8pm); admission: from 8.50 Euro; Wellnesspark, Kurbadstrasse 16; Mon–Fri 7.30 am–11 pm, Sat&Sun and publ. hols until 10 pm only; day ticket: 31.50 Euro; Tel. (both) 680 09-700; www.oberlaa.at*

behind the Museum Quarter between Siebensterngasse, Burggasse, Kirchberggasse and Stiftgasse. The land was parcelled out in the late 17th century and built on until the Biedermeier period. Its current popularity stems from a renewal programme in the 1970s. *Tram: 49; bus: 48 A; U 3, Volkstheater*

STREETS & SQUARES

Am Hof   **[110 C2–3]**

As early as the 12th century, the 'court' of the Babenberg dukes stood on this city centre site. A good 100 years later, the power base was moved to the Hofburg. The feudal flair has remained, though. Around the central Mariensäule (Maria Column), is a magnificent ensemble of façades: the Church of the Nine Choirs of Angles, to its left the Palais Collalto, where 6-year-old Mozart gave his first concert in Vienna. Opposite this, the Märklein House, by J. L. von Hildebrandt *(No. 8)* and the Bürgerliches Zeughaus (Civil Armoury) with the *Feuerwehrmu-*

seum (Fire Fighter's Museum; No. 7; Sun and publ. hols. 9 am–noon, weekdays by prior arrangement only; Tel. 531 99). Am Hof; bus: 1 A

Freyung   **[110 C2]**

The large, triangular open space in the northwest of the old town served in the Middle Ages as a market place, a stage for travelling entertainers and a place of execution all in one. On the north side, Babenberg Duke Henry II founded the Scots Monastery in 1155. Here, outside the jurisdiction of the ruler, the monastery gave sanctuary to victims of persecution – hence the name 'Freyung' which roughly means 'released from' or 'free of'. Today's monastery church dates back to the early Baroque period. Around it are a number of splendid nobleman's residences, including the Baroque Palais Daun-Kinsky, *(No. 4)* by Lukas von Hildebrandt and Palais Harrach *(No. 3)* and Palais Ferstel *(No. 2)*. Note, too, the Prior's House, nicknamed the 'Schubladenhaus' because of its resemblance to a chest of drawers! *Bus 1 A; U 3, Herrengasse*

Heiligenkreuzer Hof [111 E3]
Like many other large monasteries in Lower Austria, the Heiligenkreuz Monastery also owns a courtyard in Vienna, parts of which date back over 800 years. Today's ensemble is a product of the 18th century. Its broad central square is very quiet and idyllic. *Schönlaterngasse 5/ Grashofgasse 3; bus: 2 A*

Heldenplatz [110 B–C4]
In actual fact, the extension of the Hofburg, as planned around 1900, envisaged adding a further wing to the complex plus two arches across Ringstrasse leading to the two museums. The fall of the Habsburg monarchy, however, put an end to this gigantic project – fortunately, as it turned out, since the unique panoramic view from the semi-circular ◁▷ Neue Burg across Heldenplatz has been preserved. It takes in the long Baroque façade of the Leopoldine Wing and both grandiose equestrian statues of Archduke Charles and Prince Eugene, the Volksgarten and the outlines of City Hall and the Burgtheater as far as the Kahlenberg. The Outer Castle Gateway (1824), which separates the huge, largely grass-covered area from Ringstrasse, is by Peter von Nobile and commemorates the crushing of Napoleon at Leipzig in 1813. *Heldenplatz; tram: D, J, 1, 2; bus: 2 A; U 3, Herrengasse*

Hoher Markt [111 D2–3]
Underneath the surface of the oldest square in Vienna – the site in the Middle Ages of the dungeon, stocks and municipal law courts – remnants of foundations and walls from the Roman legion camp *Vindobona* have been discovered. The remains of the officer's quarters can be seen in an underground exhibition room *(Tues–Sun 9 am to 12.15 pm, 1 pm–4.30 pm)*.

Another attraction in the northeastern corner of the Upper Market is the *Ankeruhr* (Anchor Clock, 1911, Franz von Matsch). Incorporated into a flying buttress construction between houses No. 10 and 11, the decorative Art-Nouveau timepiece features twelve figures from the city's history, one for each hour. Every day at noon, they parade to music across the face of the clock. *Bus 2 A, 3 A; U 1, U 3, Stephansplatz*

Josefsplatz [110 C4]
This impressive square is surely the most homogeneous in the city in architectural terms. It is dominated by the front aspect of the Austrian National Library. Opposite are the Classicist Palais Pallavicini *(No. 5)* and the Palais Palffy with its Renaissance façade *(No. 6)*. *Bus 2 A*

Mariahilfer Strasse [122 A–C 1–2]
The section between the Westbahnhof station and the Museum Quarter, within the 'Gürtel', with its pleasant mixture of department stores, restaurants, bars and original shops, is ideal for a few hours' shopping. *Tram: 52, 58, 6, 9, 18; bus: 13 A, 14 A, 2 A; U 3, Zieglergasse, Neubaugasse, U 3, U 6, Westbahnhof*

Ringstrasse [110–111 B–F 1–5]
★ Having ordered that Vienna's ring of fortifications be razed to the ground in 1857, Emperor Franz Joseph had a splendid boulevard built in its place. Divided into nine

Embodiment of old democratic ideals: Athenebrunnen and Parlament

sections, it encircles the city centre and each end joins the Franz-Josefs-Kai which runs alongside the Danube Canal. This 'ring road' is 4.5 km long, 57 m wide (including both side avenues) and lined with numerous magnificent buildings, some private, some public. All these echo building styles of past eras, from Greek and Roman antiquity, the Gothic of the great cathedrals, Renaissance and Baroque down to the varied faces of Historicism. These all go together under the heading 'Ringstrassenstil'. Inaugurated on 1 May 1865, Vienna's Ringstrasse is a unique work of art in the field of urban development, unrivalled in any other European metropolis. Along some sections, pedestrians and cyclists have to share the pavement.

Strudlhofstiege   [116 C2] *Insider Tip*

The elegant staircase, whose steps and ramps mount the steep slope between Währinger Strasse and Palais Liechtenstein, came to literary fame in the German-speaking world in Heimito von Doderer's 1951 novel of the same name. Designed by Johann Theodor Jäger and built in 1910, it is lit by cast-iron, Art-Nouveau lanterns. *Strudlhofgasse, close to Liechtensteinstrasse; tram: D; bus: 40 A*

Treasures of the past

The wealth of museums and the treasures they house bear witness to the importance and power of this once imperial city

Vienna boasts over 100 museums – from world-famous collections like the Kunsthistorisches Museum, the Schatzkammer at the Hofburg or the Österreichische Galerie down to the small but nevertheless interesting memorials such as those commemorating Johann Strauss, Franz Schubert or Joseph Haydn.

This wealth of museums is due, on the one hand, to the power of the Habsburg dynasty, whose emperors enthusiastically collected paintings and other precious objects from all corners of their dominions. They employed goldsmiths and other craftsmen and they sent explorers to find and bring back treasures from all around the world.

Another reason for the varied nature of the museum landscape lies in the Viennese love of all things unusual. This is the only plausible explanation for the existence of museums dedicated to teddy bears, funerals, orthopaedic medicine, hoofed and claw-footed animals and for pathological and anatomical specimens!

Kunsthistorisches Museum: one of the world's finest art collections

The Akademie der Bildenden Künste

Most museums are closed on Mondays and on 25 December, many also on 1 May. To make up, some stay open late on one evening per week – usually Thursdays. Sunday opening times apply to public holidays as well.

Admission prices begin at 1.80 Euro (musician's memorials) and rise to 9 Euro (Museum of Fine Arts). Holders of a 'Vienna Card' are often entitled to reduced admission. Reductions of 50 per cent apply at eleven municipal museums (including the musician's memorials and the Uhrenmuseum (Clock Museum) with a joint ticket for 11.60 Euro (available at all eleven ticket offices). On Friday mornings, admission to these museums is generally free, except on public holidays.

MUSEUMS

Albertina [110 C4]

★ Situated in Augustinerstrasse, diagonally behind the Opera, the Palais Albertina is named after its founder, Duke Albert of Sachsen-Teschen, a son-in-law of Empress Maria Theresia. The building holds the largest collection of graphic art in the world. It consists of 60,000 drawings and watercolours and nearly 1.5 million prints by almost all artists of the last 600 years. Due to their sensitivity to light, these works cannot be displayed permanently. The painstakingly restored building also hosts excellent changing exhibitions. *Daily 10 am–6 pm, Wed until 9 pm; Augustinerstrasse; www.albertina.at; tram: D, J, 1, 2, 62, 65; bus: 59 A; U 1, U 2, U 4, Karlsplatz*

Akademie der Bildenden Künste [110 C5]

The Academy of Fine Arts, built in the high Renaissance style and decorated with terracotta reliefs and frescoes, is a world-famous gallery showing a representative cross-section of western painting from six centuries. Artists include Hans Baldung Grien, Lucas Cranach the Elder, Titian, Peter Paul Rubens, Rembrandt, Johannes Vermeer and Anthonis van Dyck. Centrepiece is the *Triptych of the Last Judgement* by Hieronymus Bosch, a cavalcade of fascinating yet brutal visual fantasies. The adjoining Kupferstichkabinett (Graphics Collection) consists of several hundred pictures from the Biedermeier period and medieval architectural sketches. *Tues–Sun and publ. hols 10 am–4 pm; Schillerplatz 3; tram: D, J, 1, 2; bus: 57 A; U 1, U 2, U 4, Karlsplatz*

Erzbischöfliches Dom- und Diözesanmuseum [111 D3]

The Cathedral and Diocesan Museum contains the medieval treasures of St. Stephen's, including Gothic altar panels and sculptures, relics, stained glass windows and liturgical objects. The image of Duke Rudolf IV (1365), founder of the University and sponsor of the Cathedral, is held to be the first individual portrait to be painted north of the Alps. *Tues–Sat 10 am to 5 pm; Stephansplatz 6, passage-way; U 1, U 3, Stephansplatz*

Heeresgeschichtliches Museum [124 B4–5]

The Museum of Military History tells the story of the Habsburg army and navy, from the Thirty Years' War and the war against the Turks down to the campaigns against Italy, Prussia, Hungary and World War I. Tragic centrepiece is the bloodstained uniform worn by heir to the throne Franz Ferdinand upon his assassination on 28 June 1914 in Sarajevo. *Sat–Thurs 9 am–5 pm; Arsenal/Objekt 18, tram: D, O, 18; bus: 69 A*

Hermesvilla [126 C3]

Emperor Franz Joseph gave his wife Sisi this villa in the Lainz Game Preserve as a hunting lodge. Today, the Historical Museum regularly stages interesting special exhibitions here. *Apr–Sept: Tues–Sun 10 am–6 pm; Oct–Mar: Tues–Sun and publ. hols 9 am–4.30 pm; Lainzer Tiergarten; entrance: Hermesstrasse; bus: 60 B*

Historisches Museum der Stadt Wien [111 D6]

Appearances can be deceptive: behind the unprepossessing 1950s façade to the left of the Church of St. Charles Borromeo, the Historical Museum is a highly interesting collection tracing Vienna's progress from prehistoric settlement and Roman army camp *Vindobona*, via Babenberg and Habsburg royal capital to the city of today. First-rate paintings from the Biedermeier and Art Nouveau periods, archaeological finds, Turkish 'booty' from 1683, sculptures and glass windows from St. Stephen's Cathedral, documents on the industrial and 1848 revolutions, craft objects, a model of the 19th-century city and more besides. *Tues–Sun 9 am to 6 pm; Karlsplatz; tram: D; U 1, U 2, U 4, Karlsplatz*

Silberkammer und Kaiserappartements [110 C3–4]

Only the best is good enough; the Imperial Silver Collection contains porcelain from East Asia, Sèvres and Vienna's own Augarten production, crystal glasses and silver cutlery. Highlights are the almost 30-m-long Milan Centrepiece and a splendid dinner service for 140 people. The Imperial Apartments encompass the private quarters of Emperor Franz Joseph I and his wife Elisabeth, their dining room, the great audience chamber, the imperial officers' quarters, the conference room of the crown council and council of ministers and the apartments occupied by Tsar Alexander I during the Congress of Vienna. *Daily 9 am–5 pm; Inner Courtyard, Imperial Gateway; bus: 2 A; U 1, U 3, Stephansplatz, U 3, Herrengasse*

Josephinum [116 C2]

This early Classicist building, the former Military Academy for Medicine and Surgery, today houses the Museum of Medical History. The collection documents the development of Viennese medicine from Gerard van Swieten, Maria Theresia's doctor, down to Sigmund

---

MARCO POLO Highlights »Museums«

★ **Albertina**
After a general overhaul, the largest collection of graphic art in the world (page 42)

★ **Kunsthistorisches Museum**
Tizians, Breughels, Rembrandts etc. (page 44)

★ **Museumsquartier**
Vienna's latest top attraction: the new mega culture complex (page 46)

★ **Naturhistorisches Museum**
Dinosaur skeletons, insects and the Venus of Willendorf (page 46)

★ **Österreichische Galerie**
Gustav Klimt's *Kiss* plus other highlights of Vienna Art Nouveau (page 46)

★ **Schatzkammer**
The coronation insignia and precious treasures of the Holy Roman Empire (page 48)

Freud. Note the eye-catching, life-size wax anatomical models, commissioned by Joseph II in 1785 in Florence to enable his military doctors to study human anatomy. *Mon–Fri 9 am–3 pm; Währinger Strasse 25/1; tram: 37, 38, 40–42*

Jüdisches Museum der Stadt Wien [110 C4]
The Jewish Museum has a permanent display on the religion and its often tragic history, plus changing exhibitions on topics such as literature, architecture and photography. *Sun–Fri 10 am–6 pm, Thurs 10 am to 8 pm; Dorotheergasse 11; U 1, U 3, Stephansplatz*

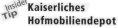

Kaiserliches Hofmobiliendepot [122 B2]
If you want to know more about how the Habsburgs lived and the story of Viennese furniture from the

Kunsthistorisches Museum, domed hall with café

17th to the 20th centuries, visit the Imperial Furniture Collection. Emphasis on Biedermeier and Historicism. *Tues–Sun 10 am–6 pm; Mariahilfer Strasse 88; entrance: Andreasgasse 7; U 3, Neubaugasse*

Kunstforum [110 C2]
Star architect Gustav Peichl designed this venue for regular, top-class changing exhibitions of 19th- and 20th-century painting. *Daily 10 am–7 pm, Fri until 9 pm; Freyung 8; tram: D, 1, 2; U 2, Schottentor, U 3, Herrengasse*

Kunst-Haus Wien [118 B4]
Some 3,500 sq m of exhibition space in colourful surroundings, part permanent Hundertwasser exhibition, part changing displays by well-known artists from all over the world. *Daily 10 am–7 pm; guided tours: Sun and publ. hols 11 am, noon; for special exhibitions 3 pm; Untere Weissgerberstrasse 13; tram: N, O*

Kunsthistorisches Museum [110 B5]
★ The Museum of Fine Arts is one of the world's great museums. Its stock of exhibits are the fruit of that passion for collecting which saw the art-loving Habsburgs systematically amass treasures from the 16th century onwards. Centrepiece is the Picture Gallery on the first floor, the fourth largest in the world. Its treasures include numerous major works by Breughel, Rubens, Rembrandt, Dürer, Raffael, Tizian, Tintoretto, Veronese, Caravaggio, Velázquez and other masters of 15th–17th-century Italian, French, Spanish and Dutch painting. Second point of emphasis is the Collection

of Sculpture and Decorative Arts, featuring precious specimens of the goldsmith's and gem cutter's art, plus ivory carvings, mechanical objects, clocks, astrological instruments and much more. The most famous items are Benvenuto Cellini's golden salt cellar, the Krumauer Madonna and Jan Vermeyen's narwhal-tusk tankard.

The magnificent Ringstrasse building, opened near the end of the 19th century, also contains a Coin Collection, a fine Egyptian and Near Eastern Collection and a Collection of Greek and Roman Antiquities. The Collections of Ancient Musical Instruments, of Arms and Armour and the Ephesus Museum are to be found in the New Palace at the Hofburg. The beautifully restored Palais Harrach is also part of the Museum of Fine Arts and is used for special exhibitions. *Main building: Tues–Sun 10 am–6 pm, Thurs until 9 pm; Burgring 5 (entrance: Maria-Theresien-Platz); tram: D, J, 1, 2; bus: 57 A; U 2, Babenbergerstrasse, U 3, Volkstheater; New Palace: Wed–Mon 10 am–6 pm; Heldenplatz (entrance: behind Prince Eugene Monument); how to get there: see main building; Palais Harrach (during special exhibitions) daily 10 am–6 pm; Freyung 3; tram: D, 1, 2; U 2, Schottentor, U 3, Herrengasse*

Insider Tip

Künstlerhaus [111 D6]
The neo-Renaissance building shows major changing exhibitions, some on international art, some on Austrian cultural history. *Fri–Wed 10 am–6 pm, Thurs 10 am–9 pm; Karlsplatz 5; tram: D, J, 1, 2, 62, 65; bus: 4 A, 59 A; U 1, U 2, U 4, Karlsplatz*

Lipizzanermuseum [110 C4]
Everything you want to know about the famous white horses of Lipica. *Daily 9 am–6 pm; Reitschulgasse 2; bus: 2 A, 3 A; U 3, Herrengasse*

Museum für Angewandte Kunst [111 F3–4]
The Museum of Applied Arts shows European arts and crafts from the Middle Ages to the present: glass, ceramics, metal, furniture, porcelain, textiles, plus objects from East Asia. The 'MAK' collection is not only rich and varied, but also very strikingly presented. Highlights are the works of the Wiener Werkstätte and the unique oriental carpets. Regular special exhibitions showcase contemporary art. *Tues 10 am to midnight, Wed–Sun 10 am–6 pm, Thurs until 9 pm; Stubenring 5; tram: 1, 2; bus: 4 A, 74 A; U 3, Stubentor*

Museum im Schottenstift [110 C2]
The art collection of the Benedictine Scots Monastery contains works from the medieval period and early modern age. The altar by the Viennese Scots Master (around 1470) shows the oldest depiction of Vienna. *Thurs–Sat 10 am–5 pm, Sun 11–5 pm; Freyung 6; tram: D, 1, 2; bus: 1 A; U 2, Schottentor*

Museum für Völkerkunde [110 B–C4]
Insider Tip

Vienna's Ethnological Museum is one of the most comprehensive of its kind. Focal points are the Captain James Cook Oceania Collection, the bronze sculptures from Benin and the ancient Mexican treasures including Montezuma's feathered crown. *Wed–Mon 10 am to 6 pm; New Palace; Heldenplatz; tram: 1, 2, D, J, 46, 49; bus: 48 A, 57 A; U 2, U 3, Volkstheater*

Museumsquartier   [110 A–B 4–5]

★ Within the renovated Baroque former imperial stables, a unique museum complex has evolved over the last few years, covering an area of 60,000 sq m. Since its opening in the summer of 2001, it has formed part of one of the largest cultural quarters in the world, together with the Museums of Fine Art and Natural History and the Hofburg. Here, the dramatic juxtaposition of Baroque and contemporary architecture is reflected in the broad spectrum of culture on offer. More than 20 museums, autonomous initiatives and projects are based here and make the Museum Quarter – MQ for short – just as much artistic laboratory and archive, as site of experimental practice and theoretical reflection, a place where art is both produced and presented.

The MQ's most significant institutions include the *Leopold-Museum,* containing the world's largest Schiele collection and major works by Gustav Klimt, Oskar Kokoschka, Herbert Boeckl, Alfred Kubin and many others. *(Mon, Wed–Sun 10 am–7 pm, Tues&Fri until 9 pm),* and the *Museum Moderner Kunst* (Museum of Modern Art), where modern classics, post-war Austrian avant-garde and the most important current artistic trends such as Informal, photo realism, object- and action painting are showcased *(Tues–Sun 10 am–6 pm, Thurs until 10 pm).*

Next door are the main building of the *Kunsthalle,* the *Architek-turzentrum Wien,* the *Tanzquartier Wien,* the *Tobacco Museum,* the *Zoom Children's Museum* including a theatre *(changing opening hours and programmes; Mon–Fri approx. 9 am–4 pm, Sat&Sun, publ. hols and school hols approx. 10 am; info: Tel. 524 79 08; www.kinder museum.at).* Two large halls and experimental areas are available for initiatives in the field of film, new media and art theory.

Thanks to a total of ten entrances and passageways plus numerous gastronomic outlets, the MQ also serves as an attractive linking element between the historical city centre and the surrounding districts, and as a meeting place and pulsating hub of night-time activity. *Museumsplatz 1; Tel. 523 58 81; www.mqw.at; tram: 49; bus: 2 A, 48 A; U 2, U 3, Volkstheater or Babenbergerstrasse*

Naturhistorisches Museum   [110 A–B4]

★ From dinosaur skeletons to the world's largest collection of insects (over 6 million specimens), from the 26,000-year-old stone statue, the Venus of Willendorf, to meteorites, precious stones and a huge collection of skulls – the splendid Natural History Museum on Ringstrasse is one of the largest in Europe. *Thurs–Mon 9 am–6.30 pm, Wed 9 am–9 pm; Burgring 7; entrance: Maria-Theresien-Platz; tram: D, J, 1, 2, 46, 49; bus: 48 A; U 3, Volkstheater*

Österreichische Galerie   [123 F3]

★ The Austrian Gallery in the Upper Belvedere features 19th- and 20th-century art, first and foremost regional classics of the Biedermeier

Can the elephants at the Naturhistorisches Museum still flap their ears?

period (Ferdinand Georg Wald-müller, Rudolf von Alt) via late Romantics and *Gründerzeit* (Leopold Kupelwieser, Hans Makart) down to Art Nouveau, Expressionism and the post-war period (Egon Schiele, Oskar Kokoschka). In addition, major international art, including Caspar David Friedrich, Claude Monet, Vincent van Gogh, Auguste Rodin, Emil Nolde and Edvard Munch. The No. 1 crowd-puller is, however, Gustav Klimt, in particular, his *Kiss*.

The Lower Belvedere houses the Museum mittelalterlicher Kunst (Museum of Medieval Art) and the *Barockmuseum* (Baroque Museum), which shows a cross-section of visual and plastic arts from the late 17th to late 18th centuries. Highlights: the amusing busts by Franz Xaver Messerschmidt, the original lead figures from Georg Raphael Donner's fountain, pictures by Johann Michael Rottmayr and Franz Anton Maulpertsch. *Tues to Sun 10 am–7 pm; Oberes Belvedere: Prinz-Eugen-Strasse 27; tram: D; Unteres Belvedere: Rennweg 6A; tram: 71*

Österreichisches Theatermuseum   [110 C4]

Some 1.5 million exhibits make the Austrian Theatre Museum, in the magnificent Palais Lobkowitz, the largest in the world. The permanent exhibition, just a fragment of what's on offer, is backed up by numerous special shows. *Tues–Sun 10 am–5 pm, Wed 10 am–8 pm (guided tours by prior arrangement: Tel. 512 88 0-0); Lobkowitzplatz 2, tram: D, J, 1, 2; bus: 3 A; U 1, U 2, U 4, Karlsplatz*

Pathologisch-Anatomisches Bundesmuseum   [116 C2]

Not for the faint-hearted, but symptomatic of the darker side of the Viennese soul! Deformed skeletons, cancer-ridden lungs in formalin, wax models of tumours and a collection of gall- and kidney stones – on show in the so-called 'Narrenturm' or 'Fool's Tower', the former 18th-century refuge for the mentally ill. *Wed 3 pm–6 pm, Thurs 8 am–11 am, 1st Sat in month 10 am–1 pm; Altes Allgemeines Krankenhaus; Spitalgasse 2, entr.: Van-Swieten-Gasse; tram: 5, 33, 43, 44*

Puppen- und Spielzeugmuseum [111 D2]
Charming private collection of dolls and toys. *Tues–Sun and publ. hols 10 am–6 pm; Schulhof 4; U 1, U 3, Stephansplatz*

Schatzkammer [110 C4]
★ One of the most valuable treasure collections in the world can be marvelled at in the Secular and Ecclesiastical Treasuries. It includes the insignia of the Holy Roman Empire, such as feudal sword, sceptre, imperial crown and sword, the so-called inalienable Habsburg heirlooms, the Burgundian treasures, the treasures of the Order of the Golden Fleece and much more. *Wed–Mon 10 am–6 pm; Hofburg/Schweizerhof; tram: D, J, 1, 2; bus: 2 A, 57 A*

Schatzkammer des Deutschen Ordens [111 D3–4]
Austria's second most important treasure house: the Treasury of the Teutonic Order of Knights holds insignia of the order, Mass requisites, ceremonial vessels, precious oriental weapons and a viper tongue credenza for detoxifying poisoned foods. *Mon, Thurs&Sun 10 am–noon, Wed, Fri&Sat 3 pm to 5 pm; Nov–Apr: daily, except Fri&Sun; Singerstrasse 7; bus: 2 A; U 1, U 3, Stephansplatz*

Technisches Museum [120 C3]
Recently re-opened after years of renovation work, the venerable Museum of Technology looks at this complex cultural phenomenon and its development as a part of our everyday life. The steam engine gallery and the realistic representation of a coal mine are of particular interest. *Mon–Sat 9 am–6 pm, Thurs 9 am–8 pm, Sun 10 am to 6 pm; Mariahilfer Strasse 212; tram: 58, 52, 10; bus: 10 A; U 4, Schönbrunn*

MEMORIALS

Over the centuries, many great creative figures have been associated with Vienna. Several of the houses in which they were born, lived or died have been turned into commemorative memorials. Opening times, unless otherwise stated, are as follows: *Tues–Sun 9 am–12.15 pm, 1 pm–4.30 pm*

Beethoven-Gedenkstätten
Born in Bonn in Germany, Ludwig van Beethoven lived for much of his life in Vienna, moving house some 60 times! His three most famous addresses are the Eroica-Haus, where he composed his third symphony, *Eroica*, in 1803–04; the Pasqualatihaus, in which he wrote the opera *Fidelio*, and the Heiligenstädter-Testament-Haus. Here, in 1802, he drew up his famous will – 'Testament' in German – in which he admitted to his fear of going deaf. *Eroica-Haus* [112 C4]: *Döblinger Hauptstrasse 92; Testament-Haus* [113 D1]: *Probusgasse 6 (both houses: tram: 37; bus: 38 A); Pasqualatihaus* [110 B2]: *Mölker Bastei 8; tram: D, 1, 2; U 2, Schottentor*

Figaro-Haus [111 D–E3]
The only remaining Mozart residence is a charming late Baroque house in which he spent his supposedly happiest years from 1784–87. At his desk in a wonderful stuccoed room Amadeus Mozart composed, among many other

Museums with a Difference

Symptomatic of the Viennese love of the weird and wonderful

Alongside the (world-)famous art and scientific collections, Vienna's over 100 museums include some which are dedicated to the more curious side of life. To find museums here for fire-fighters, fiacres or wine cultivation is almost to be expected. It seems rather grotesque, however, to find that the Viennese, in love with all things past, also have museums featuring bricks and heating systems, teddy bears, bells, coffins, clown's paraphernalia and the language of Esperanto! And, hidden away in the 16th district, there is even a Museum of Electropathology, dedicated to injuries caused by electricity! *For more information, see the 'Museums' brochure published by the Vienna Tourist Board.*

works, his *Marriage of Figaro*. *Tues–Sun 9 am–6 pm; Domgasse 5; U 1, U 3, Stephansplatz*

Sigmund-Freud-Museum [11 / D2]

The rooms in which the father of psychoanalysis held his surgery for almost half a century – until he was forced to leave the city in 1938 – now contain manuscripts and other memorabilia. The famous couch is, unfortunately, not among these. *Daily 9 am–5 pm; Berggasse 19; tram: D, 37, 38, 40–42; bus: 40 A*

Haydn-Wohnhaus [122 B3]

The oldest representative of the Viennese Classic style spent twelve years in this house in the suburbs until his death in 1809. Here, Joseph Haydn wrote both his oratorios *The Creation* and *The Seasons*. A memorial to Johannes Brahms, who lived in Vienna from 1869 until his death in 1897, can also be visited

here. *Haydngasse 19; bus: 57 A; U 3, Zieglergasse*

Arnold-Schönberg-Center [111 E6]

Changing exhibitions on the innovative twelve-tone composer. Occasional concerts. *End of June to Sept: Mon–Fri 10 am–5 pm; Oct to End of June: Tues–Sun 10 am to 5 pm, Thurs until 7.30 pm; Schwarzenbergplatz 6 (entrance: Zaunergasse 1–3); tram: D, 1, 2, 71; bus: 4 A*

Schubert-Geburtshaus [112 C6]

The master of song composition was born in this typical old Viennese suburban house on 31 January 1797. The house also includes a memorial to Adalbert Stifter. *Nussdorfer Strasse 54; tram: 37, 38*

Strauss-Gedenkstätte [118 B3]

It was here that the 'King of the Waltz' wrote his 'hit', *Blue Danube* in 1867. *Praterstrasse 54; U 1, Nestroyplatz*

Enjoy your meal, Viennese style

The Beisl, the café and the Heuriger – together more than ever the epitome of a warm Viennese welcome

Paris has its bistros, Madrid its bodegas, Prague its beer taverns and London its pubs. Vienna, on the other hand, has three types of typical gastronomic establishment on offer: the coffee house, the Beisl and the Heuriger.

The literature on the subject of Viennese coffee houses could fill whole libraries. As far back as the Biedermeier era, and especially around 1900, the cafés were the focal point of Viennese intellectual life. Since time immemorial, as Alfred Polgar wrote, they served 'people who wanted to be alone, but in company' – as a kind of public living room, if you like!

Today, scattered across the city, more than 500 of these oases can be found, where you can sit for hours in peace over a 'Melange' – a mocha with lots of milk – and the obligatory glass of Viennese spring water, and where there is not only a large selection of newspapers, but also chess boards, bridge cards or even billiard tables to help you while away the time. The classic

Pavement cafés
spring up out of nowhere
in fine weather

'Viennese breakfast' is served everywhere: a pot of coffee or tea plus bread rolls with butter, jam or honey and a boiled egg. During the day, in addition to various cakes and gateaux, many places serve snacks such as sausages or toasts, omelettes or goulash soup. Many of the larger, more famous cafés in the city centre are also full-blown restaurants, serving excellent meals.

The second bastion of the Viennese way of life is the 'Beisl', the traditional inn, today more popular then ever, thanks to the incredible rejuvenation process taking place in Viennese cuisine which combines Bohemian, Hungarian, Italian, Jewish and other central European culinary traditions. For decades, the city of schnitzel, *Tafelspitz*, *Beuschel*, dumplings and *Palatschinken* was pooh-poohed by gourmets for its high-calorie, high-fat fare. Meanwhile, a new generation of ambitious chefs has adapted the traditional dishes to modern-day eating habits. Several Viennese gourmet temples have even been awarded a 'chef's hat' by stern restaurant critics.

The third Viennese institution enjoys undiminished popularity: the 'Heuriger'. These traditional wine taverns, mostly with picturesque vaulted ceilings, courtyards and gardens, in which you can savour the new wines and good home cooking – often to the sound of live Viennese music – are to be found concentrated in the old wine-making villages on the outskirts of the Vienna Woods in the northwest of the city.

Just as popular are those in the quieter wine-growing regions such as Strebersdorf and Stammersdorf right up in the north on the other side of the Danube, or, close to the southern city boundary, in the district of Mauer.

The genuine Heuriger, also known as a 'Buschenschank', can be recognised by the 'Föhrenbusch', the sprig of Scots pine and the sign saying 'Ausg'steckt' by the entrance.

ICE-CREAM PARLOURS

Tichy   [123 F6]
The Mecca for friends of tasty ice creations lies a little off the beaten track in the Favoriten Quarter but it's worth the trip. Thirty flavours of ice-cream, including apricot dumpling ice, nut, fruit and chocolate 'Busserln' (kisses)! *Mid-Mar to Sept: daily; Reumannplatz 13; U 1, Reumannplatz*

Eissalon Tuchlauben   [111 D3]
The very finest *gelato italiano*! Ideal location for city strollers on the edge of the pedestrian zone. *End of Mar–Sept: daily; Tuchlauben 15; bus: 2 A, 3 A; U 1, U 3, Stephansplatz*

HEURIGER

Augustinerkeller   [110 C4]
In the original vaulted cellars of this traditional tavern you'll find classic Heuriger fare, from *Stelze* to schnitzel and *Gspritzte*. *Daily; Augustinerstrasse 1; Tel. 533 10 26; tram: D, J, 1, 2; U 1, U 2, U 4, Karlsplatz*

Hermann   [126 C3]
An alternative to the much-visited district of Grinzing: pleasant garden with vine bower. *Mar–Nov: daily, except Wed; Jan&Feb: Sat&Sun only 3.30 pm–11 pm; Johann-Staud-Strasse 51; Tel. 914 81 61; bus: 46 B, 146 B*

Mayer am Pfarrplatz   [113 D1]
Classic Heuriger, with large courtyard and garden – and lots of famous-name guests. Very cosy. Beethoven composed his ninth symphony here. *Mon–Sat 4 pm to midnight, Sun and publ. hols from 11 am; Pfarrplatz 2; Tel. 370 12 87; bus: 38 A*

Reinprecht   [126 C2]
Large tavern, steeped in tradition, in a former monastery. Fifteen rooms and large garden. Prize-winning home-produced wines. Largest cork collection in Austria. *Mar–mid-Nov: daily 3.30 pm to midnight; Cobenzlgasse 22; Tel. 320 14 71; bus: 38 A*

Sirbu   [127 D2]
★ ◁/▷ Drink and dine amidst vineyards, with a fabulous panoramic view of Vienna. *Mid-Apr–mid-Oct: Mon–Sat 3 pm–midnight; Kahlenberger Strasse 210; Tel. 320 59 28; bus: 38 A, then on foot or by taxi*

COFFEE HOUSES & CAKE SHOPS

Bräunerhof [110 C4]

Refined, drawing-room atmosphere, waiters with greying hair, live chamber music on weekday afternoons, international newspapers. Even the eternally bad-tempered Thomas Bernhard felt at home here. *Daily; Stallburggasse 2; bus: 2 A, 3 A; U 1, U 3, Stephansplatz*

Café Central [110 C3]

Magnificent café now resurrected in the Venetian/neo-Gothic style. The finest men of letters and journalists of the late 19th and early 20th century sharpened their quills here, so to speak. Terrace. *Daily, except Sun evenings; Herrengasse 14; bus: 1 A; U 3, Herrengasse*

Dommayer [120 A4]

Traditional establishment with fine garden in the heart of posh Hietzing district. Ideal after a visit to Schloss Schönbrunn. *Daily; Dommayergasse 1; tram: 58, 60; U 4, Hietzing*

Frauenhuber [111 D4] *Insider Tip*

Vienna's oldest café is a real gem, with Persian carpets, red plush upholstery and Biedermeier display cabinets. *Daily; Himmelpfortgasse 6; U 1, U 3, Stephansplatz*

Hawelka [110–111 C-D3]

★ ✗ The Bohemian clientele of old has given way largely to students

---

MARCO POLO Highlights
»Food & Drink«

★ **Hawelka**
Vienna's Bohemian café par excellence (page 53)

★ **Schnitzelwirt**
Hearty stuff: the biggest schnitzel in town (page 59)

★ **Griechenbeisl**
Vienna's oldest restaurant with original autographs of Mozart and Beethoven on the walls (page 55)

★ **Hietzinger Bräu**
Viennese beef tradition at its finest (page 55)

★ **Kurcafé Oberlaa**
Magnet for the sweet-toothed; the best pastries for miles around (page 57)

★ **Lusthaus**
Dine in true Biedermeier style – in the heart of the Prater (page 57)

★ **Wrenkh**
Paradise for dyed-in-the-wool vegetarians (page 57)

★ **Gulaschmuseum**
Classic paprika dish in 15 varieties (page 56)

★ **Kunsthalle Café**
Where Vienna's movers and shakers dine – well into the night if need be (page 59)

★ **Sirbu**
The epitome of the Heuriger, with Viennese panorama (page 52)

and tourists. Yet the cosy, almost claustrophobic atmosphere, thick with cigarette smoke, and the hot *Buchteln* – served after 10 pm – are still the same as ever. *Mon, Wed to Sat 8 am–2 am, Sun 4 pm–2 am; Dorotheergasse 6; bus: 3 A; U 1, U 3, Stephansplatz*

Hold [116 B4]

🏃 In the tiny café-bar you'll find an excellent espresso, and the pasta is served in an almost genuine Italian ambience. *Daily, except Sun; Josef-städter Strasse 50; tram: J*

Korb [111 D3]

Pleasantly unpretentious café-restaurant, popular artists' haunt. *Daily, except in the morning on Sun and publ. hols; Brandstätte 9; U 1, U 3, Stephansplatz*

Landtmann [110 B2]

◁▷ Large, classic and admittedly expensive Ringstrasse café, used during the week by politicians, journalists and business people as a sort of 'second office' and it is always crowded in the evening. In the summer, pretty terrace. *Daily; Dr.-Karl-Lueger-Ring 4; tram: 1, 2, D, 37, 38, 40–44; bus: 1 A; U 2, Schottentor*

Museum [110 C5–6]

Corner café designed by Adolf Loos, with clear, understated atmosphere. The favourite meeting place for Bohemians and chess players – and, sadly, very smoky. *Daily, except Sun; Friedrichstrasse 6; tram: 62, 65; U 1, U 2, U 4, Karls-platz*

Sperl [117 D6]

Traditional café, full of atmosphere, with billiard tables and cosy niches. *Mon–Sat 7 am–11 pm, Sun and publ. hols 11 am–8 pm; July&Aug: daily, except Sun; Gumpendorfer Strasse 11; bus: 57 A*

Many cafés still preserve something of their 19th-century atmosphere

Guide to Viennese Coffee

**There's more than one way
to make coffee in Vienna**

To be precise, Viennese coffee houses offer you at least twelve variations of coffee. To start with, there's the small or large 'Schwarze' (mocha without milk) or 'Braune' (with milk). The 'Melange' is coffee with lots of milk, topped with a little 'Schlagobers' (whipped cream) and dusted with either coffee, cinnamon or cocoa powder. A 'Kaisermelange' has an egg yolk stirred in! The 'Fiaker' is a glass of mocha, the 'Einspänner', a Fiaker with a portion of whipped cream. A coffee diluted with added water is a 'Verlängerter'.

RESTAURANTS €€€

Griechenbeisl [111 E3]
★ Refined menus at Vienna's oldest restaurant – over 500 years old – located in a vaulted cellar. The big attraction is the Mark Twain Room (or Signature Room); prominent guests from Mozart and Beethoven to Einstein and Gina Lollobrigida have signed their names on the walls and ceiling. *Daily; Fleischmarkt 11; Tel. 533 19 41; U 1, U 4, Schwedenplatz*

Hietzinger Bräu [120 A4]
★ Here, not only the *Tafelspitz* is first-rate. In their extremely elegant main restaurant, Ewald Plachutta and his team serve more than a dozen dishes featuring boiled beef with such wonderful names as 'mageres Meisel', 'Hüferschwanzel', 'weisses Scherzl', 'Kruspelspitz', served in the proper fashion in a beef bouillon or with apple and horseradish sauce, fried potatoes and chive sauce. *Daily; Auhofstrasse 1; Tel. 877 70 87; tram: 58, 60; U 4, Hietzing*

Schnattl [116 C4] *Insider Tip*
Very cosy, up-market Beisl serving excellent food, equally good wines and with extremely attentive service. Tables also in the pleasant garden. *Daily; except Sat&Sun; Lange Gasse 40; Tel. 405 34 00; tram: J*

Zu den drei Husaren [111 D4]
Steeped in tradition and in exquisite taste. Period furniture, candlelight, waltz music and perfect service go to make the right framework for the glorious kitchen creations. *Daily; Weihburggasse 4; Tel. 512 10 92 0; U 1, U 3, Stephansplatz*

RESTAURANTS €€

Altes Fassl [123 D3] *Insider Tip*
An extremely welcoming restaurant. Traditional Viennese cuisine, including roast chicken, steak and fried onions and *Tafelspitz*. Idyllic garden terrace. *Daily, except Sat lunchtime; Ziegelofengasse 37; Tel. 544 42 98; bus: 13 A, 59 A; U 4, Pilgramgasse*

Gourmet Restaurants in Vienna

Korso bei der Oper   [111 D5]

Not without reason is this gourmet temple worth three chef's hats in the opinion of the stern critics at Gault-Millau. Whether it's old-Viennese, such as potato goulasch or fried entrails, or experimental, such as ray or morel ravioli, what the chef de cuisine Reinhard Gerer conjures up in the restaurant of the Hotel Bristol is among the best that new Austrian cuisine has to offer. The wine list, too, is exceptional. Menu from 55 Euro; *daily, except Sat lunchtime; July: also Sun lunchtime; Mahlerstrasse 2; Tel. 515 16-546; tram: 1, 2, D, J; U 1, U 2, U 4, Karlsplatz*

Palais Schwarzenberg   [123 F2]

Can there be a more charming setting for a dinner than the winter garden in the old field-marshal's palace, with its view over the Baroque park? Discrete elegance is the watchword; ambience and quality of both service and food are outdone only by the impressive prices. The cuisine is refined, with many French dishes and the wine cellar nothing less than superb. Lunch is to be had from a reasonable 30 Euro. *Daily; Schwarzenbergplatz 9; Tel. 798 45 15-600; www.palais-schwarzenberg.com; tram: D*

Steirereck   [118 C5]

This magnificently appointed restaurant gets top marks in all the gastronomic guide books. The Reitbauer family, their head chef Helmut Österreicher and sommelier Adi Schmid conjure up night after night a culinary work of art unrivalled in the whole of Austria. The prices are correspondingly steep. But wait a moment! The three-course lunch costs an amazing 35 Euro. In the evening, main courses start at around 65 Euro. *Daily, except Sat&Sun; Rasumofskygasse 2; Tel. 713 31 68; tram: N*

Grünauer   [122 B1]

A Viennese eating establishment in the best sense of the word. The wine list reads like a wine-grower's Debrett's Peerage and the head chef has the art of traditional old-Austrian cooking off to a T. The regular diners are of the same pedigree and prominence as the menu! *Daily, except Mon lunchtime and Sat&Sun; Hermanngasse 32; Tel. 526 40 80; tram: 49; bus: 13 A, 48 A*

Gulaschmuseum   [111 E3]

★ A 'museum', though of a different kind: no less than 15 variations of the famous Hungarian paprika and meat speciality are on the menu. In summer you can eat outside. *Daily; Schulerstrasse 20; Tel. 512 10 17; U 1, Stephansplatz*

Kornhäuslturm   [111 D2]

Good, solid fare in pseudo Art-Nouveau interior with reasonably-priced lunchtime menu. Terrace. *Daily;*

FOOD & DRINK

Fleischmarkt 1 A; Tel. 535 59 36; bus: 2 A; U 4, Schwedenplatz

Kurcafé Oberlaa [111 D4]

★ City centre branch of the cake shop at the spa resort Oberlaa, renowned for its delicious cakes and gateaux. The open sandwiches, salads and savoury strudel variations are also to die for – ideal as a snack in between meals, especially in fine weather when you can sit outside. *Daily 8 am–8 pm; Neuer Markt 16; Tel. 513 29 36; bus: 3 A; U 1, U 3, Stephansplatz*

Lusthaus [127 E3]

★ ⁂ A pretty, former imperial hunting lodge with a terrace, complete with tall chestnut trees, pretty waitresses and sparkling wines. On warm summer evenings, amidst the Prater meadows, this combination will transport you to seventh heaven! The fact that the kitchen is fully capable of satisfying even the most sophisticated tastes only heightens the pleasure. *Sat&Sun, publ. hols noon 6 pm, Apr–Oct. also Mon, Tues, Thurs&Fri noon to 11 pm; Freudenau 254 (main avenue); Tel. 728 95 65; bus: 77 A*

Insider Tip
Schlossgasse 21 [122 C3]

Old-Viennese culinary delights from egg dumplings to *Tafelspitz* in a romantic vaulted cellar or the idyllic garden. Clientele tend to be chic, including many media people. Excellent selection of local wines and fruit schnapps. *Daily 6 pm–3 am; Schlossgasse 21; Tel. 544 07 67; bus: 13 A, 59 A; U 4, Pilgramgasse*

Witwe Bolte [116 C5–6]

Venerable and cosy old inn with garden in the Biedermeier quarter.

The food is typically Viennese and hence not for the figure-conscious – but very tasty indeed! *Daily, lunchtime and evenings; in summer in fine weather open all day; Gutenberggasse 13; Tel. 523 14 50; tram: 49; U 3, Volkstheater*

Wladimir [122 A2]

Palmeni, Sakuska, Borschtsch – genuine Russian cooking of a high standard and in authentic surroundings. *Daily, except lunchtimes and Mon; Bürgerspitalgasse 20; Tel. 595 25 24; U 3, U 6, Westbahnhof*

Wrenkh

★ Vienna's pioneer and master of healthy eating is a Mecca for vegetarians. With its chic bar, the city-centre branch is fashionable; the other version is more laid-back. *Daily; Bauernmarkt 10; Tel. 533 15 26; U 1, U 3, Stephansplatz* **[111 D3]** *and Servitengasse 14; Tel. 319 77 63; U 4, Rossauer Lände* **[117 D2]**

Zu den Drei Buchteln [122 C3]

Head chef, Vratislav Krivak, is a credit to his Bohemian name. The likes of the truly genuine *Grammelknödel* (bacon dumplings), *Powidltascherln* and excellent Pilsener or Budweiser served in this wood-panelled restaurant is seldom found in Vienna. *Daily, except lunchtimes and Sun; Wehrgasse 9; Tel. 587 83 65; bus: 13 A, 59 A*

Inigo [111 E3]

Friendly, easy-going meeting place for a mixed bag of guests. Specialities: spare-ribs and vegetarian menus. *Mon–Sat 8.30 am–mid-*

Vienna Specialities

Tuck into these delicacies!

Apfelstrudel – a dream of a dessert, consisting of grated apple, chopped nuts, sultanas, flavoured with cinnamon and sugar, in wafer-thin flaky pastry

Beuschel – small pieces of innards, (mostly heart and lung) in a spicy sauce

Buchteln – yeast-risen pastry (Dampfnudeln), shaped like dumplings, filled with jam and often served with vanilla sauce

Frankfurter – the sausages, which are otherwise known as 'Wiener Würstchen', surprisingly enough

Frittaten – egg pancakes, fried in fat and cut into thin strips. Served in clear, beef bouillon

Powidltascherln – Bohemian pastry dish, a sweet speciality consisting of potato pastry cases filled with stewed plum

Kaiserschmarrn – dessert made of torn or shredded pancakes, sprinkled with sultanas and sugar and covered in stewed plum sauce

Nockerln – not unlike Italian *gnocchi* – these dumplings, made with semolina or butter, find their way into soups, or with whisked egg become the legendary 'Salzburger Nockerln'

Palatschinken – sweet pancakes, filled, in the classic style, with

apricot jam (Marillenmarmelade). There are also widely-available variations which are filled with quark (Topfen), chocolate sauce or ice-cream

Sachertorte – addictive substance for chocaholics: the ultimate gateau, made from egg yolk, sugar, a little flour and stiffly beaten egg whites, sandwiched together with apricot jam and covered with a layer of chocolate

Stelze – grilled lower leg of pork or veal; typically served with sauerkraut and bread dumplings

Tafelspitz mit G'röste – prime piece of boiled beef, thickly sliced and generally accompanied by chive sauce, fried potatoes and apple or bread sauce with horseradish

Wiener Schnitzel – direct descendent of the 'costoletta milanese', the classic veal cutlet, coated in breadcrumbs and fried golden brown. Ideal accompaniment: potato salad

night, Sun and publ. hols 10 am to 4 pm; July&Aug: daily, except Sat&Sun; Bäckerstrasse 18; Tel. 512 74 51; U 3, Stubentor

Schnitzelwirt [122 B1]

★ A household name among taxi drivers and those Viennese with an enormous appetite. Décor and service are irrelevant; the schnitzel are bigger and cheaper than anywhere else! *Daily, except Sun; Neubaugasse 52; Tel. 523 37 71; tram: 49; bus: 2 A, 13 A, 48 A*

Schweizerhaus [118 C3]

A Wurstelprater institution. Hearty, old-Viennese cooking, from schnitzel and mirror carp to *Schweinsstelze* and gulasch. In summer, you can sit outside in the shade of the huge chestnut trees. *Mid-Mar–Oct: daily; Prater 116; Tel. 728 01 52; tram: 21; U 1, Praterstern*

Suppe & Co. [122 B1]

The city's No. 1 soup specialist. Old-Viennese and international delicacies and home-made noodle dishes. *Daily, except Sat&Sun; Neubaugasse 5; Tel. 523 83 13; bus: 13 A; U 3, Neubaugasse*

Ubl [123 D2]

For the nostalgic at heart: wooden floors and panelling, old-fashioned iron stove and a bar from way back when. Tasty, solid fare. Terrace open in the summer. *Daily; Pressgasse 26; Tel. 587 64 37; bus: 59 A; U 4, Kettenbrückengasse*

Café Stein [110 B1]

🏃 Student café offering breakfast, good food and an internet bar turns

must-visit 'in' bar in the evening. Then, mostly Italian drinks and espressi go down best. *Mon–Fri 7 am–1 am, Sat&Sun 9 am–1 am; Währinger Strasse 6–8; Tel. 319 72 41; tram: 37, 38, 40–44; U 2, Schottentor*

Gräfin vom Naschmarkt [110 B6]

Lifeline for night-owls who suddenly have a craving for goulash soup or other hearty dishes. *Daily 4 am–2 am; Linke Wienzeile 14; Tel. 586 33 89, U 4, Kettenbrückengasse*

Krah-Krah [111 E2]

Vienna's top meeting place for beer freaks – more than 50 different sorts available here. The Krah Krah is one of the pioneers of the so called Bermuda Triangle in the northeast of the city centre and is correspondingly well-frequented. There's much jostling at the bar even early in the evening. The interior is both excruciatingly smoky and excruciatingly loud, the atmosphere and the guests very much in keeping with the 'scene'. In summer, you can sit outside. *Mon–Sat 11 am–2 am, Sun and publ. hols 11 am–1 am; Rabensteig 8; Tel. 533 81 93; bus: 2 A; U 1, U 4, Schwedenplatz*

Kunsthalle Café [110 C6]

★ Simple, posh and arty; DJs every day; good food. In summer, enjoy the view of the Church of St. Charles Borromeo from the large garden. Even after its re-vamp, still a popular scene meeting place, with trendy art exhibitions on the premises. *Daily 10 am–2 am; Treitlstrasse 2; Tel. 586 98 64; U 1, U 2, U 4, Karlsplatz*

Shopping in style

**Antiques, Tracht, Augarten porcelain:
Vienna may not be cheap,
but tasteful souvenirs are guaranteed**

The metropolis on the Danube is pricey, especially when it comes to international brand-name accessories and fashions.

A more interesting prospect are the local, traditional products – items in gold, silver or enamel, *Tracht* (traditional costumes), *Loden* wear, fine glassware, wines, made-to-measure suits and shoes, Biedermeier or Art-Nouveau materials. For a classic souvenir, look no further than Augarten porcelain, petit point embroidery and the legendary *Sachertorte*. The pawnbroker's and auctioneer's Dorotheum never ceases to amaze, where you can browse for hours to your heart's content. The so called ★ *Antiques Quarter,* between the Hofburg and St. Stephen's Cathedral **[110–111 C–D 3–4]** is a collector's paradise. More than two dozen shops sell a wide range of items, everything from Gothic angels and Baroque cupboards down to affordable, second-hand gifts.

A surprising number of small and unusual shops are to be found in the side streets, most notably in the 8th (Josefstadt), 7th (Neubau) and 6th (Mariahilf) districts. The major shopping streets in the centre

Top address: 'E. Braun & Co.' on the Graben

Colourful goings-on at the flea market

are Graben, Kohlmarkt and Kärntner Strasse; then there are of course the pedestrian zones. Here you'll find most of the old, traditional top addresses which still bear the title of 'K. & K. Hof' (Royal and Imperial Court) or even 'Kammerlieferant' (Purveyor to the Sovereign) on their company plaque. Their wonderfully old-fashioned elegance in itself makes them worth a visit.

Less aristocratic – but consequently a lot cheaper – are the shops in the big shopping streets, most importantly Mariahilfer Strasse, the far end of Favoritenstrasse and Landstrasser Hauptstrasse. The department stores, with the possible exception of Steffl and the Ringstrassengalerien arcade, are not an absolute must on a classic shopping itinerary.

Many shops are open until 7 or 8 pm on weekdays; on Saturdays doors close at 5 pm at the latest.

Dorotheum

Over 200 years of tradition make this pawnbroker's an institution for art lovers and collectors

Furniture, carpets, porcelain, coins, books, stamps, weapons, jewellery, toys, all manner of curios and, above all, art in all price and quality classes are to be had here. You can either buy items in the conventional manner or bid for them at an auction. Such objects are displayed for one week, bearing the estimated value determined by the valuer. *Mon–Fri 10 am to 6 pm, Sat 9 am–5 pm; information and auction catalogues: Tel. 515 60-212; Dorotheergasse 17; bus: 2 A, 3 A; U 1, U 3, Stephansplatz* **[110 C4]**

ACCESSORIES & JEWELLERY

Hartmann **[111 D4]**
Hand-made spectacles of international renown. Plus combs, shoehorns, etc. made of horn. Highly original shop window displays. *Singerstrasse 8; U 1, U 3, Stephansplatz*

Heldwein **[111 D3]**
One of the big names among Viennese up-market jewellers. *Graben 13; bus: 2 A, 3 A; U 1, U 3, Stephansplatz*

Horn
Robert Horn designs and manufactures tasteful accessories and travel goods in leather; timeless, elegant and perfectly crafted. *Bräunerstrasse 7; U 1, U 3, Stephansplatz* **[110 C3]***; Mahlerstrasse 5; U 1, U 2, U 4, Karlsplatz* **[111 D5]**

Köchert **[111 D4]**
Viennese jewellery from avant-garde to classical. *Neuer Markt 15; U 1, U 3, Stephansplatz*

Michaela Frey **[110 C4]**
Here you'll find luxurious and decorative enamel jewellery set in 24-carat gold. *Lobkowitzplatz 1; tram: D, J, 1, 2; U 1, U 2, U 4, Karlsplatz*

Phoenix **[110 B2]**
Whether it's a conventional tie, bow tie, cap, pair of braces or a gentlemen's waistcoat, tasteful hand-made items are the trademark of this house – the oldest tie-maker's in the city. *Schottengasse 4; tram: D, 1, 2, 37, 38, 41–44; U 2, Schottentor*

Schullin **[110 C3]**
Chic, up-to-the-minute jewellery design. The entrance, created by Hans Hollein, is an attraction in its own right. *Kohlmarkt 7; bus: 2 A, 3 A; U 3, Herrengasse*

ANTIQUES & ANTIQUARIAN BOOKS

Asenbaum **[111 D4]**
Good-quality furniture, paintings, silver, glassware, porcelain and jewels. *Kärntner Strasse 28; tram: D, J, 1, 2; U 1, U 2, U 4, Karlsplatz*

Christian Nebehay [111 D5]
Books and art, above all from the Art Nouveau and Secession eras. *Annagasse 18; tram: D, J, 1, 2; U 1, U 2, U 4, Karlsplatz*

Gilhofer [110 C3]
One of the leading sources of all things Austrian, such as prints, books and maps, plus scientific material. *Bognergasse 2; bus: 1 A; U 1, U 3, Stephansplatz*

Reinhold Hofstätter [110 C4]
Classic art and antique dealer. High-quality paintings, sculptures, furniture, arts and crafts from the Gothic period to the early 19th century. *Bräunerstrasse 12; U 1, U 3, Stephansplatz*

Wiener Antiquariat [111 D4]
★ One of the best addresses for topographical views of Austria, rare prints and books. *Seilergasse 16; bus: 3 A; U 1, U 3, Stephansplatz*

Zacke [110 C3]
Specialist for Asian art of all kinds. *Wallnerstrasse 4; U 3, Herrengasse*

DELICATESSEN & WINE

Culinarium Österreich [111 D4]
★ Delicacies from the different federal states, to sample and buy. Restaurant and wine dealers. *Neuer Markt 7; U 1, U 3, Stephansplatz*

Grams & Co. [111 E4]
A large range of top Austrian wines – and the odd rarity to be discovered, too. *Singerstrasse 26; U 1, U 3, Stephansplatz*

Keck's Feine Kost [110 C3]
The No. 1 for Austrian delicacies, ham from South Tyrol, woodland honey from South Styria, plus home-made jam, cheese, sausage, paté, pickled vegetables, oil and wine. *Herrengasse 15; U 3, Herrengasse*

MARCO POLO Highlights
»Shopping«

★ **Altmann & Kühne**
Sweet souvenirs
(page 67)

★ **Culinarium Österreich**
Delicacies from the federal states (page 63)

★ **Antiques Quarter**
The old, the beautiful, the unusual (page 61)

★ **Naschmarkt**
Vienna's finest food 'bazaar' (page 65)

★ **Resi Hammerer**
Austrian look: 'Tracht' fashions (page 65)

★ **Steffl**
Leads the way in fashion and lifestyle (page 64)

★ **Vinissimo**
Fine wines from Austria (page 64)

★ **Wiener Antiquariat**
Beautiful prints of old Vienna (page 63)

Meinl am Graben [110 C3]
The best delicatessen in the city, now with its own excellent restaurant. *Graben 19; bus: 2 A, 3 A; U 1, U 3, Herrengasse*

Vinissimo [110 A6]
★ First-class wines from all over Austria. You can sample them, too, over a snack in the tiny bistro. *Mon–Sat 11 am–11 pm; Windmühlgasse 20; bus: 2 A, 57 A*

GALLERIES

Curtze [111 D4]
Contemporary art from Austria. Emphasis on Actionists such as Brus, Nitsch or Rainer. *Tues–Fri 11 am–6 pm, Sat 11 am–4 pm; Seilerstätte 15–16; tram: 1, 2; U 1, U 3, Stephansplatz*

Faber [123 E3]
Vienna's top address for international photographic art. *Tues–Fri 2 pm to 6 pm, Sat 11 am–5 pm; Brahmsplatz 7; U 1, Taubstummengasse*

Grita Insam [111 E3]
Trendsetter in all things avant-garde. *Tues–Fri noon–6 pm, Sat noon–5 pm; Köllnerhofgasse 6; bus: 2 A; U 1, U 3, Stephansplatz*

Krinzinger [111 D4]
Brand new works and traditional favourites from home and abroad. *Tues–Fri noon–6 pm, Sat 11 am to 4 pm; Seilerstätte 16; tram: 1, 2; U 1, U 3, Stephansplatz*

GLASS

Bakalowits [111 D3]
From crystal ashtrays, silver and porcelain to chandeliers for the drawing room! *Spiegelgasse 3, on the corner with Graben; bus: 3 A; U 1, U 3, Stephansplatz*

Kovacek [111 D4]
Finest quality antique glassware from Gablonz to Lalique. *Spiegelgasse 12; bus: 3 A; U 1, U 3, Stephansplatz*

Lobmeyr [111 D4]
Exquisite crystal chandeliers, mirrors, glasses. In-house glass museum. *Kärntner Strasse 26; U 1, U 3, Stephansplatz*

DEPARTMENT STORES

Gerngross [122 C1]
Department store with 180 years of service. Mid-range prices and a huge selection over five floors. *Mon–Fri 9.30 am–7 pm, Sat 9 am to 5 pm; Mariahilfer Strasse 38–48; U 3, Neubaugasse*

Haas-Haus [111 D3]
One of the most disputed buildings in Vienna. Post-modern temple to consumerism by star architect Hans Hollein; the interior is dedicated to international fashion. *Stephansplatz 12; U 1, U 3, Stephansplatz*

Ringstrassengalerien [111 D5]
Stylish shopping arcade with 70 shops over 10,000 sq m. *Kärntner Ring 5–7; tram: D, J, 1, 2, 71; U 1, U 2, U 4, Karlsplatz*

Steffl [111 D4]
★ Bags of tradition, the store was re-opened in 1998 under the banner of 'First Fashion Department Store'. Fashion and lifestyle over 12,000 sq m. Exclusive and expensive. *Mon–Fri 9.30 am–7 pm,*

Sat 9.30 am–5 pm; Kärntner Strasse 19; U 1, U 3, Stephansplatz

for many Viennese. Sat, publ. hols 6.30 am–6 pm; in ...ter: until dusk

CLASSIC SOUVENIRS

Insider Tip Augarten
The filigree statuettes and tableware from Europe's second-oldest porcelain manufacturers are among the most popular souvenirs of Vienna. The factory at Schloss Augarten offers one-hour guided tours illustrating the production process. *Tours begin Mon–Fri 9.30 am; Obere Augartenstrasse 1* **[117 F1]**; *showrooms also at Stock-im-Eisen-Platz 3–4; U 1, U 3, Stephansplatz* **[111 D3]** *and Mariahilfer Strasse 31; bus: 2 A* **[110 A6]**

Maria Stransky **[110 C4]**
Finest petit point embroidery – you can't get much more Viennese than this! *Hofburg-Passage 2; U 1, U 3, Stephansplatz, U 3, Herrengasse*

Resi Hammerer **[111 D4]**
★ *Tracht*, country and city fashions in sportingly elegant 'Austrian Look'. *Kärntner Strasse 29–31; U 1, U 3, Stephansplatz*

Trachten Tostmann **[110 B2]**
Tracht costumes for the whole family – to buy and to rent. *Schottengasse 3A; tram: D, 1, 2; U 2, Schottentor*

MARKETS & FLEA MARKETS

Flea Market **[122 C6]**
Every Saturday, the 'Fetzentandler', as the second-hand dealers are called in Vienna, set up their stalls near the U-Bahn station Kettenbrückengasse. Rummaging around here is a favourite Saturday pastime

Naschmarkt **[123 D1–2]**
★ Quintessentially Viennese with a smattering of the Balkans thrown in! The largest and probably most attractive food market in the city, stretching over 500 m – a feast for all the senses. *Along the Wienzeile, between Kettenbrückengasse and Karlsplatz; Mon–Fri 6 am–6.30 pm, Sat 6 am–5 pm; U 4, Kettenbrückengasse*

FASHION

Braun & Co. **[111 D3]**
International designer fashions for him and her in costly surroundings. *Graben 8; U 1, U 3, Stephansplatz*

Guys & Dolls **[111 D2]**
Chic things for the youth of today. *Schultergasse 2; bus. 2 A, 3 A*

Helmut Lang **[111 D4]**
Austrian pioneer on the frontiers of international design dresses the style-conscious woman and man. *Seilergasse 6; bus: 3 A; U 1, U 3, Stephansplatz*

**Humana Retro –
Trend & Jugend** **[116 B5]**
Vienna's most exciting second-hand clothing store has all the fashion highlights of the last eight decades. Whatever your mood, you'll find something that fits, from spotted bell-bottoms and crazy frilly shirts to great-grandma's lace-up corset or the scantiest hot-pants. And everything is cheaper than it looks, too. *Lerchenfelder Strasse 48; tram: 46*

Knize [111 D3]
Probably Vienna's best gentlemen's tailor. Original Adolf Loos interior. *Graben 13; bus: 2 A, 3 A; U 1, U 3, Stephansplatz*

Wolford Flagship Store [111 D4]
Top-quality underwear by this successful global company from the Vorarlberg region. *Kärntner Strasse 29; U 1, U 3, Stephansplatz*

THIS & THAT

Huber & Lerner [111 D4]
Visiting cards, wedding cards and fine stationery. *Weihburggasse 4; U 3, Stephansplatz*

Lambert J. Hofer [125 D5]
Costumes and elegant evening wear for hire. *Simmeringer Hauptstrasse 28; Tel. 740 90-0; tram: 71, 72,*

Retti [110 C3]
Jewellery, watches, candles. The building was designed by Hans Hollein. *Kohlmarkt 10; bus: 2 A, 3 A; U 3, Herrengasse*

Schönbichler [111 D3]
Vienna's leading tea specialist. Over 100 different blends from all over the world, in a fitting, colonial-style interior. *Wollzeile 4; bus: 2 A; U 1, U 3, Stephansplatz*

Walter Weiss [122 C1]
Hundreds of different hand-crafted hair and clothes brushes to last a lifetime. *Mariahilfer Strasse 33; bus: 2 A*

Zauberklingl [111 D5]
Magic tricks, joke articles and fireworks. *Führichgasse 4; tram: D, J, 1, 2; bus: 3 A; U 1, U 2, U 4, Karlsplatz*

MUSIC, RECORDINGS & FILMS

Doblinger [110 C4]
Old, established source of new and second-hand scores. Specialist

A throwback to the days of Empire: Schönbichler's tea shop on the Wollzeile

music literature, records. *Doro-theergasse 10; U 1, U 3, Stephans-platz*

Satyr [111 D2]
Large film dealers, including some 20,000 English-language videos, plus a huge range of relevant books. *Vorlaufstrasse 5; tram: 1, 2; U 4, Schwedenplatz*

Teuchtler [110 A6]
Treasure trove for collectors. Second-hand classical, pop and jazz records and CDs. *Windmühlgasse 10; bus: 2 A, 57 A*

INTERIOR DECORATORS

Backhausen [111 D4]
Exquisite furnishing and decorative materials, designer furniture, gifts, home accessories with the emphasis on Art Nouveau. *Kärntner Strasse 33; tram: D, J, 1, 2; U 1, 11 2, 11 4, Karlsplatz*

Galerie Ambiente [111 D3]
Superlative Art-Nouveau furniture. *Lugeck 1; bus: 2 A; U 1, U 3, Stephansplatz*

Hartmann Henn [110 C3]
Designer furniture and original souvenirs. *Naglergasse 29; bus: 1 A; U 3, Herrengasse*

Karolinsky [111 D4]
Art-Nouveau and Art-Déco designer lamps along the lines of Josef Hoffmann, Adolf Loos, Kolo Moser, among others. *Singerstrasse 16; U 1, U 3, Stephansplatz*

Wittmann [110 C6]
Top-class upholstered furniture from the drawing boards of such

stars as Paolo Piva, Matteo Thun and Josef Hoffmann. *Akademiehof, Friedrichstrasse 10; tram: D, J, 1, 2; U 1, U 2, U 4, Karlsplatz*

SHOES

Ludwig Reiter [110 B2]
Classic, elegant, hand-crafted footwear over 350 sq m from this Viennese shoe manufacturer. Everything from gentlemen's shoes and half-boots to specialist models for golfing, mountaineering and hiking. *Mölkersteig 1; tram: D, 1, 2; U 2, Schottentor*

Materna [111 D5]
Budapester brogues and similar classic made-to-measure footwear. Expensive, but made to last a lifetime. *Mahlerstrasse 5; tram: D, J, 1, 2; U 1, U 2, U 4, Karlsplatz*

CONFECTIONERY

Altmann & Kühne [111 C3]
★ Sweets, handmade chocolate, and mini confectionery, packed in charming little boxes. *Graben 30; bus: 2 A, 3 A; U 1, U 3, Stephansplatz*

Demel [110 C3] Insider Tip
Finest boxes of chocolates and cakes made by the former Royal and Imperial Court Confectioner's. *Kohlmarkt 14; bus: 2 A; U 3, Herrengasse*

Sacher [110–111 C–D5]
Birthplace of the most famous Viennese sweet, the *Sachertorte*. Buy one to take with you, or have one sent – anywhere in the world. *Kärntner Strasse 38; tram: D, J, 1, 2; U 1, U 2, U 4, Karlsplatz*

A bed for
the night

**Whether on the slopes of the Vienna Woods,
or at a stylish city-centre address –
we've got the best tips for a good night's sleep**

As Vienna graduated to become one of Europe's top destinations, the hotel industry responded by drastically increasing the number of beds in the 1980s and 1990s. International chains have built a number of big, new hotels in the city, particularly in the four- and five-star categories. Numerous historical buildings, too, from Gründerzeit palaces on the Ringstrasse to grain warehouses along the Danube, have been renovated and turned into mostly luxurious hotel accommodation. Many old established mid-range houses have been modernised and extended, generally preserving their nostalgic flair. Today, over 40,000 beds in around 400 establishments are available to guests.

The range of facilities and quality of service has also been raised to meet international standards, resulting in a leap in prices. An attractive luxury room in the inner city will set you back on average 110 Euro. If that goes far beyond your budget, you'll have to be prepared to accept less. You'll

Pure 'Royal and Imperial' nostalgia: Vienna's famous Hotel Sacher decked out to welcome its guests

scarcely find a bed for under 50 Euro, except in a youth hostel.

Hotels and guesthouses in Vienna are assigned to one of five categories, from five-star luxury hotel to modest guesthouse with only one star. The mid range three-star establishments offer decently furnished rooms, with or without bath or shower and toilet. A peculiarity of Vienna are its guesthouses. These are mostly small-scale affairs, individual in character and located in residential or office blocks. In contrast to conventional hotels, the emphasis is on a bed and breakfast service, and they are often run by the owners themselves. They generally do not have a restaurant.

In the summer, cheap accommodation is to be had in so called seasonal hotels, student halls of residence which function as hotels during the summer holidays from 1 July to 30 September. An alternative, even for a short stay, is to rent an apartment. These usually have separate living and sleeping quarters and their own cooking facilities. Service is, however, very limited. In the case of longer stays, cheaper flat rates are charged.

Vienna's popularity as both a holiday destination and on the international conference circuit means it is advisable to book your room in advance, especially in the high season, that is from May to October and over the Christmas period. A list of all hotels is available free of charge from the Vienna Tourist Board. The prices quoted in the brochure are not always one hundred per cent correct. This is also the case with the prices given at any one time on the internet under *www.info.wien.at.*

Individual travellers can take advantage of the reservation service offered by the Vienna Tourist Board and book their accommodation from home *(daily 9 am–7 pm; Tel. 01-245 55; www.info.wien.at)*. Seasonal hotel rooms are available via the *Österreichische Hochschülerschaft (Tel. 310 88 80-0)*. Young people looking for cheap accommodation in student residences usually strike lucky with the *Hochschülerschaft der Uni Wien (Mon to Fri 9 am–2 pm; Tel. 585 69 69-33; www.oeh.ac.at)*.

If you arrive in Vienna and have to start looking for a room, the *Tourist Information Offices* can help you to find a hotel to suit your needs. Prices include VAT, service charge, heating surcharge and all other taxes. In most cases, these are official prices, but if you turn on the charm while booking or on arrival at reception, you might be able to negotiate a discount!

HOTELS €€€

Cordial Theater-Hotel Wien   [116 B–C4]

★ Plush, solid four-star hotel. Not exactly cheap, but charming and likeable. *54 rooms; 1080 Vienna, Josefstädter Strasse 22; Tel. 405 36 48; Fax 405 14 06; chwien@cordial.co.at; tram: J; bus: 13 A*

Dorint Biedermeier Wien   [118 B5]

★ If you want to sample the charms of early 19th-century Vienna, this is the place for you. Renovated some years ago, at great cost and with a real sense of style, the complex is now a comfortable four-star hotel including an idyllic courtyard, the only one of its kind in Europe to have survived intact from the Biedermeier era. *203 rooms; 1030 Vienna, Landstrasser Hauptstrasse 28; Tel. 716 71-0; Fax 716 71-503; dorint.biedermeier@dorint.com; bus: 74 A; U 3, Rochusgasse*

Hilton Vienna Danube   [127 E3]

★ ⬃ This unprepossessing giant block on the banks of the Danube used to be a grain warehouse. It offers not only unusually generous rooms, but also a unique view of the river. A little outside the city centre, but with good transport links to the airport, the exhibition grounds and the Prater. The hotel's own shuttle service takes you into the city centre in ten minutes. *367 rooms; 1020 Vienna, Handelskai 269; Tel. 727 77; Fax 727 77-199; info_vienna-danube@hilton.com; tram: 21; bus: 83 A, 84 A, 80 B*

König von Ungarn   [111 E3]

Atmospheric and more like a private city residence, the König von Ungarn (The King of Hungary) is just a minute's walk from St. Stephen's Cathedral. The furnish-

MARCO POLO **Highlights**
»Accommodation«

★ **Dorint Biedermeier Wien**
Enjoy the flair of the 19th-century, but with 20th-century comfort (page 70)

★ **Strandhotel Alte Donau**
Friendly, down-to-earth hotel with its own bathing beach (page 76)

★ **Schlossherberge Wilhelminenberg**
Probably the best youth hostel location in Europe (page 77)

★ **Hotel Wandl**
Elegant and welcoming, reasonably priced and in an unbeatable location (page 75)

★ **Cordial Theater-Hotel Wien**
Plush, solid four-star hotel (page 70)

★ **Pension Arenberg**
Refined, intimate Ringstrasse hotel (page 74)

★ **Appartements in der Josefstadt**
Furnished apartments: ideal for a longer stay in Vienna (page 76)

★ **Rathaus**
Unpretentious, close to the centre and cheap (page 76)

★ **Hilton Vienna Danube**
Hotel in former grain warehouse (page 70)

ings are discreet and sophisticated. Note the charming foyer – with elegant bar – in the glass-roofed inner courtyard. *33 rooms; 1010 Vienna, Schulerstrasse 10; Tel. 515 84-0; Fax 515 84-8; hotel@kvu.at; bus: 2 A; U 1, U 3, Stephansplatz*

Parkhotel Schönbrunn [120 A4]
Opened at the beginning of the 20th century, Franz Joseph's pompous guesthouse rated as one of the world's most fashionable hotels. A touch of its imperial splendour lives on, and modern side wings have been added. Its proximity to the Schönbrunn palace and park compensates for its location, a little outside the centre in the up-market district of Hietzing (ten minutes by U-Bahn into the centre), but does mean that the hotel can get fairly crowded. *399 rooms, 1130 Vienna, Hietzinger Hauptstrasse 10–20; Tel. 878 04; Fax 878 04-32 20; parkhotel.schoenbrunn@austria-trend.at; tram: 10, 58; U 4, Hietzing*

Das Triest [123 D2] *Insider Tip*
The former stables of the Royal and Imperial mail coach service have been turned, with much attention to detail, into an up-to-date five-star hotel by London designer Terence Conran. A real gem! *73*

Luxury Hotels in Vienna

Grandhotel Wien   [111 D5]

Five-star hotel combining today's high standards of modern facilities and creature comforts with the opulence and spaciousness of the belle époque, situated in the heart of the City. *208 rooms; from 370 Euro; 1010 Vienna, Kärntner Ring 9; Tel. 515 80-0; Fax 515 13 12; reservation@grand hotelwien.com; tram: D, J, 1, 2, 62, 65; U 1, U 2, U 4, Karlsplatz*

Bristol   [111 D5]

A fin-de-siècle hotel, with original furnishings: plenty of marble, gold, velvet and silk – and a guest list packed with big names from the world of high society and culture. Fabulous location opposite the Opera House. The Korso restaurant is one of the finest in the country. *140 rooms; from 345 Euro; 1010 Vienna, Kärntner Ring 1; Tel. 515 16-0; Fax 515 16-550; hotel.bristol@westin.com; tram: D, J, 1, 2, 62, 65; U 1, U 2, U 4; Karlsplatz*

Im Palais Schwarzenberg   [111 E6]

This Baroque palace in its huge landscape park is a truly unique hotel, satisfying the highest standards. The extensive grounds are just a stone's throw from Ringstrasse and the Opera House, yet manage to create a welcome sense of distance to the frantic world outside. *36 rooms and suites; from 265 Euro; 1030 Vienna, Schwarzenbergplatz 9; Tel.* *798 45 15; Fax 798 47 14; reser vierung@palais-schwarzenberg. com; tram: D, 71; U 4, Stadtpark*

Imperial   [111 D5–6]

Austria's top hotel plays host to the republic's most illustrious official guests. Built towards the end of the 19th century as a city residence for the Duke of Würt-temberg, this huge building, with its ceiling frescoes, sumptuous carpets, old paintings, fine period furniture and its marble staircase constitutes a magnificent, lived-in museum. In addition, it rates as one of the top culinary addresses in Vienna. *138 rooms; from 510 Euro; 1015 Vienna, Kärntner Ring 16; Tel. 501 23-0; Fax 501 10-440; hotelimperial@luxury collection.com; tram: D, J, 71, 1, 2; U 1, U 2, U 4, Karlsplatz*

Sacher   [110–111 C–D5]

The hotel, like the chocolate cake which bears its name, is a symbol of Vienna. Directly behind the Opera House, it was already an institution in the days of empire, thanks, on the one hand, to its luxurious furnishings and, on the other, to its famous cigar-smoking owner, Anna Sacher. Divided into both rooms and suites, it houses one of the finest private art collections in the city. *108 rooms; from 312 Euro; 1010 Vienna, Philharmonikerstrasse 4; Tel. 514 56; Fax 514 56-799; wien@sacher. com; tram: D, J, 1, 2; U 1, U 2, U 4, Karlsplatz*

rooms; 1040 Vienna, Wiedner Hauptstrasse 12; Tel. 589 18-0; Fax 589 18-18; back@dastriest.at; tram: 62, 65; U 1, U 2, U 4, Karlsplatz

HOTELS €€

Benediktushaus [110 C6]

Insider Tip

Just about as central a location as you can get: the guesthouse at the venerable Schottenstift (Scots Monastery). It's quiet too, thanks to the monastery courtyard, and the contemplative atmosphere is added to by the hotel's own chapel. *21 rooms; 1010 Vienna, Freyung 6A; Tel. 53 49 89 00; Fax 53 49 89 05; benediktushaus@schottenstift.at; bus: 1 A; U 2, Babenberger Strasse*

Fürstenhof [116 A6]

Pleasant family hotel opposite the Westbahnhof (railway station);

Fitting welcome for honoured guests: staircase at the Hotel Imperial

73

handy for visitors arriving by train. *58 rooms; 1070 Vienna, Neubaugürtel 4; Tel. 523 32 67; Fax 523 32 67-26; reception@hotel-fuerstenhof.com; tram: 6, 9, 18; U 3, U 6, Westbahnhof*

Graben [111 D3]
Four-star hotel in the heart of Vienna with bags of atmosphere and good service. *41 rooms; 1010 Vienna, Dorotheergasse 3; Tel. 512 15 31; Fax 512 15 31-20; graben@kremslehnerhotels.at; U 1, U 3, Stephansplatz*

Ibis Wien [122 A3]
First-class, sometimes a little turbulent, popular with groups. *341 rooms; 1060 Vienna, Mariahilfer Gürtel 22–24; Tel. 599 98; Fax 597 90 90; h0796@accor-hotels.com; tram: 6, 18; U 3, U 6, Westbahnhof, U 6, Gumpendorferstrasse*

Insider Tip **Landhaus Fuhrgassl-Huber** [126 C2]
Exclusive country house situated on the edge of the vineyards in the picturesque wine-growing village of Neustift am Wald. From here it's just ten minutes' walk to the Vienna Woods; the bus into the city takes around 20 minutes. *38 rooms; 1190 Vienna, Rathstrasse 24; Tel. 440 30 33; Fax 440 27 14; fuhrgassl-huber@hotels.or.at; bus: 35 A*

Mercure Secession [110 C6]
A popular choice with anybody who's anybody in the singing world and prefers to avoid the usual five-star stop-overs; from opera stars to musical artists from the nearby Theater an der Wien. Discretion and style are the watchwords of the house. *68 rooms and apartments; 1060 Vienna, Getreidemarkt 5; Tel. 588 38-0; Fax 58 83 82 12; h3532@accor-hotels.com; tram: D, J, 1, 2; bus: 57 A; U 1, U 2, U 4, Karlsplatz*

Novotel Wien West [126 B3]
International-standard accommodation on the outskirts of the city. Set in spacious grounds, it even has its own outdoor swimming pool! Handy for guests arriving by car along the A1 highway from the west who want to avoid driving through the city centre. *116 rooms; 1140 Vienna, Am Auhof; Tel. 979 25 42-0; Fax 979 41 40; h0521@accor-hotels.com; bus: 151*

Opernring [110 C5]
This hotel is brimming with old Viennese charm and occupies a prime location opposite the Opera House. *35 rooms; 1010 Vienna, Opernring 11; Tel. 587 55 18; Fax 587 55 18 29; reservation@opernring.at; tram: D, J, 1, 2; bus: 57 A; U 1, U 2, U 4, Karlsplatz*

Park-Villa [112 B5]
Intimate, Art-Nouveau ambience at this well-kept four-star hotel in Döbling, Vienna's most exclusive residential area. Just a ten-minute bus ride into the city centre. *21 rooms; 1190 Vienna, Hasenauerstrasse 12; Tel. 367 57 00; Fax 367 57 00-41; office@.parkvilla.at; bus: 37 A, 40 A*

Pension Arenberg [111 F3]
★ This elegant, cosy guesthouse is conveniently situated on the edge of the old town, not far from the Danube Canal. *22 rooms; 1010 Vienna, Stubenring 2; Tel. 512 52 91;*

Fax 513 93 56; arenberg@eunet.at; tram: 1, 2; U 3, Stubentor

Pension Nossek [110 C3]

Well looked-after, family-run guesthouse, just two minutes' walk from St. Stephen's Cathedral in the pedestrian zone. Typical Viennese charm. *26 rooms; 1010 Vienna, Graben 17; Tel. 533 70 41; Fax 535 36 46; reservation@pension-nossek.at; bus: 1 A, 2 A, 3 A; U 1, U 3, Stephansplatz*

Regina [110 B1]

Renowned high-end hotel in a huge 19th-century building. Well-placed, close to Ringstrasse and next to the Votivkirche. *127 rooms; 1096 Vienna, Rooseveltplatz 15; Tel. 404 46-0; Fax 408 83 92; reservierung@kremslehnerhotels.at; tram: 37, 38, 40 to 42; U 2, Schottentor*

**Rosen-Hotel
Am Augarten** [118 B2]

This hotel is situated between the two green city oases, the Augarten and the Prater. Friendly, bright and immaculate. *65 rooms; 1020 Vienna, Heinestrasse 15; Tel. 214 35 07; Fax 214 35 07-81; augarten@austria-hotels.co.at; tram: 21; U 1, Praterstern*

Hotel Wandl [111 D3]

★ This elegant, family-run hotel dates back to 1700. It has been renovated and boasts an unbeatable central location: Graben and St. Stephen's Cathedral are just a stone's throw away. Some rooms have no en-suite bathroom, however, and car drivers must use public car parks, since the hotel has no garage. *138 rooms; 1010 Vi-*

enna, Petersplatz 9; Tel. 534 55-0; Fax 534 55-77; reservation@hotel-wandl.com; bus: 2 A; U 1, U 3, Stephansplatz

Zur Wiener Staatsoper [111 D5]

Solid, middle-class family hotel in a 19th-century building. Small, but with a pleasant atmosphere and every modern convenience. Thanks to its central location, the main sights are practically on the doorstep. *22 rooms; 1010 Vienna, Krugerstrasse 11; Tel. 513 12 74; Fax 513 12 74-15; office@zurwienerstaatsoper.at; tram: D, J, 1, 2; U 1, U 2, U 4, Karlsplatz*

HOTELS €

Gabriel [124 C3]

Quietly situated, medium sized, pleasant hotel. All rooms have TV and a telephone. Hotel car park. *40 rooms; 1030 Vienna, Landstrasser Hauptstrasse 165; Tel. 712 67 54; Fax 712 67 54-10; office@hotel-gabriel.at; bus: 74 A; tram: 18; U 3, Schlachthausgasse*

Hotelpension Kraml [122 B2]

Relaxed, two-star hotel in quiet location, close to the Westbahnhof (railway station). *14 rooms; 1060 Vienna, Brauergasse 5; Tel. 587 85 88; Fax 586 75 73; pension.kraml@chello.at; bus: 57 A*

Kärntnerhof [111 E3]

Right in the historic heart of Vienna, less than three minutes from the Steffl department store. A comfortable old hotel; no frills, but cosy all the same. *43 rooms; 1010 Vienna, Grashofgasse 4; Tel. 512 19 23; Fax 513 22 28 33;*

www.karntnerhof.com; U 1, U 3,
Stephansplatz

Kolping-Gästehaus [122 C2]
A mere two minutes' walk from
the Naschmarkt and approximately
five minutes from Ringstrasse. Conveniently situated, practical and
impeccably run. *29 rooms; 1060
Vienna, Gumpendorfer Strasse 39;
Tel. 587 56 31; Fax 586 36 30;
reservierung@wien-zentral.kolping.
at; bus: 57 A; U 4, Kettenbrückengasse*

Kugel [122 B1]
Reasonably-priced, modest hotel. A
little run down, perhaps, but cheap
and close to the picturesque Biedermeier quarter on the Spittelberg.
*38 rooms; 1070 Vienna, Sieben-
sterngasse 43; Tel. 523 33 55; Fax
523 33 55-5; office@hotelkugel.at;
tram: 49; bus: 2 A, 13 A*

Pension City [111 D3]
Quiet bed and breakfast guesthouse
with stylish, comfortable rooms.
Located on the second floor of
the house where dramatist Franz
Grillparzer was born, just two
minutes from St. Stephen's Cath-
edral. *19 rooms; 1010 Vienna,
Bauernmarkt 10; Tel. 533 95 21;
Fax 535 52 16; welcome@citypen
sion.at; bus: 2 A, 3 A; U 1, U 3,
Stephansplatz*

Pension Falstaff [117 D2]
Simple, but cosy accommodation,
halfway between the Danube
Canal and the Palais Liechtenstein.
Shared showers on the landing.
Approximately 15 minutes' walk
into the city centre. *17 rooms;
1090 Vienna, Müllnergasse 5;
Tel. 317 91 27; Fax 31 79 18 64;*

pension-falstaff@gmx.at; bus: 40 A;
tram: D

Pension Neuer Markt [111 D4]
A modern and comfortable guesthouse in a prime location, about
halfway between the State Opera
House and St. Stephen's Cathedral.
*37 rooms; 1010 Vienna, Seilergasse
9; Tel. 512 23 16; Fax 513 91 05;
hotelpension.neuer.markt@aon.at;
bus: 3 A; U 1, U 3, Stephansplatz*

Rathaus [116 C4]
★ Pleasant, reasonably-priced hotel
in the centre of the old Viennese
district of Josefstadt, close to City
Hall. *8 apartments; breakfast not
included (self-catering accommodation); 1080 Vienna, Lange Gasse
13; Tel. 406 01 23; Fax 408 42 72;
hotelrathaus@gmx.at; tram: J; bus:
13 A; U 3, Lerchenfelder Strasse*

Strandhotel Alte Donau [127 D2]
★ Friendly, family-run hotel not far
from UN City on the edge of the
Alte Donau recreational area. Just a
few minutes by U-Bahn from the
city centre. The hotel even has its
own bathing beach and sunbathing
lawn! *33 rooms; 1220 Vienna, Wagramer Strasse 51; Tel. 204 40 40;
Fax 204 40 40-40; office@strand
hotel-alte-donau.at; tram: 25; U 1,
Alte Donau*

**Apartements
in der Josefstadt** [116 B3]
★ Sixteen individually furnished
apartments in an old Viennese town
house. Prices: per person per day:
62 Euro; per week: from 220 Euro.
*1080 Vienna, Alser Strasse 29/
Kochgasse 36; Tel. 406 51 12; Fax*

406 51 12-13; apartments.josef stadt@chello.at; tram: 5, 33, 43, 44; bus: 13 A

Fleger [126 C3]

The Fleger family offers ten cosy, four-star flats, between 40 and 60 sq m, situated right in the centre of the archetypal Viennese suburb of Ottakring. Long-stay discounts are also available. Prices: per person per day: 62 Euro for two people sharing. *1160 Vienna, Seitenberggasse 19, Tel. 406 51 62, Fax 406 51 62-10; office@fleger.at; tram: J, 44*

YOUTH HOSTELS & SEASONAL HOTELS

You can stay at a youth hostel for a maximum of three nights. If you do not have a Youth Hostel Association pass, you have to pay a surcharge of 3 Euro per day.

Sommerhotel Don Bosco [125 D2]

Seasonal hotel, open from 1st July to 30th September. Simple but satisfactory accommodation; all rooms have a shower and toilet. A popular choice with cyclists, as it has storage facilities for bicycles in the cellar and is located just five minutes' ride from the Prater. Price: 37–56 Euro, including breakfast; *44 rooms; 1030 Vienna, Hagenmüllergasse 33; Tel. 711 84-555; Fax 71 18 41 12; sommerhotel@ donbosco.at; bus: 79 A; U 3, Kardinal-Nagl-Platz*

Jugendgästehaus Hütteldorf-Hacking [126 C3]

Youth guesthouse set in spacious grounds with parking facilities for guests. Located in the green belt, in the western Wien valley, close to the Lainz Game Preserve, yet just 15 minutes from the city centre. Open all year round. 307 beds; single rooms to eight-bed dormitories. From 14 Euro, including breakfast. *1130 Vienna, Schlossberggasse 8; Tel. 877 15 01; Fax 87 70 26 32; jgh@verkehrs buero.at; bus: 53 B; U 4, Hütteldorf*

Jugendherberge Wien Myrthengasse [116 B5]

Friendly, modern and in tip-top condition. Open all year round. 260 beds; double rooms to six-bed dormitories. From 15.50 Euro, including breakfast. *1070 Vienna, Myrthengasse 7/Neustiftgasse 85; Tel. 523 63 16-0; Fax 523 58 49; hostel@chello.at; bus: 48 A*

Porzellaneum [117 D2]

Simple accommodation, but close to the city centre. Open from July to September. Price: 18 Euro per person in single or double room. *51 rooms; 1080 Vienna, Porzellangasse 30; Tel. 317 72 82; Fax 317 72 82-30; office@porzellan eum.sth.ac.at; U 4, Rossauer Lände*

Schlossherberge Wilhelminenberg [126 C3]

★ ◁◁▷ Europe's 'Youth Hostel with the finest view' stands in a huge park in the Vienna Woods with a panoramic view of the city. The only disadvantage therefore is the 20-minute trip into the city centre. Open all year round. 41 four-bed rooms. Price (YHA members): 18 Euro, including breakfast. *1160 Vienna, Savoyenstrasse 2; Tel. 485 85 03-700; Fax 485 85 03-702; shb@verkehrsbuero.at; bus: 46 B, 146 B*

Late-night programme for every taste

Sublime arias and monologues, cheeky pub comics, musicals or techno – on Vienna's cultural scene, the word 'boredom' doesn't exist

There's a lot going on in Vienna. Since awakening from its post-war slumbers in the late 1970s, Vienna's cultural and entertainment scene has advanced to become almost as varied as that of Paris or London. Naturally enough, Vienna owes its world-wide reputation as a highly sophisticated metropolis to its major attractions, the State Opera, the Musikverein and the Konzerthaus. Here, the stages are peopled by a constant stream of the crème de la crème of serious music. The Burgtheater still rates as one of the leading German-language stages – despite the moaning and groaning which went on during Claus Peymann's 13-year directorship, which ended in the summer of 1999.

Alongside all this, the city offers a wealth of other varied events, a fact which a glance at the weekly listings magazines *Falter* and *City* or the relevant pages of the daily newspapers will confirm. Whether it be light comedy or vicious polit-

Live music and hot rhythms at Jazzland

ical cabaret, an evening of arias or a heavy-metal concert, musical hits or experimental theatre, there's something to entertain everyone.

During the peak months of July and August, however, many cultural temples are closed, most notably the four large state-run theatres. To make up for this, such events as the 'KlangBogen' or the Music Film Festival on the Rathaus-platz, plus countless theatre and operetta festivals, concerts and readings are staged around Vienna – ideal for summer excursions.

BARS & MUSIC CLUBS

Arena   **[125 E3]**
🏃 Well-established alternative venue for everything from rock oldies and punk to reggae and techno. *Baumgasse 80; bus: 80 A; U 3, Erdberg*

B 72   **[116 A3]** *Insider Tip*
🏃 No food, but they do serve up occasional live acts, from electro to rock. *Daily 8 pm–4 am; Stadtbahn-bogen 72; U 6, Alser Strasse*

Blue Box [122 B1]

🏃 Club music, 1970s, ska etc. Different DJ every day. Good food. *Tues–Thurs&Sun 10 am–2 am, Fri&Sat 2 am–4 am; Richtergasse 8; bus: 13 A; U 3, Neubaugasse*

Bockshorn Irish Pub [110 C3]

The pioneer among Vienna's now numerous Guinness 'filling stations'! Small, great atmosphere, also recommended to whiskey drinkers. *Mon–Sat 4 pm–2 am, Sun and publ. hols 6 pm–midnight; Naglergasse 7; bus: 1 A; U 3, Herrengasse*

Insider Tip **Chelsea** [116 A5]

🏃 Rock, house, break beat, Britpop and indie – plenty of people, loud music and great DJs. *Mon–Sat 6 pm to 4 am, Sat 4 pm–4 am; Lerchenfelder Gürtel 29–31/U-Bahn archway; U 6, Thaliastrasse*

Donau [116 C6]

🏃 Not exactly the epitome of cosiness, but extremely hip and kitted out with one of the longest bars in town. *Daily 8 pm–4 am; Karl-Schweighofer-Gasse 10; tram: 49; bus: 2 A; U 2, Museumsquartier*

Eden-Bar [111 D4]

Up-market haunt of the conservative gent and countless VIPs whose famous faces grace the windows onto the street. Ties compulsory! Live music. *Daily 10 pm–4 am; Liliengasse 2; U 1, U 3, Stephansplatz*

Flex [117 E3]

★ 🏃 Underground live in a U-Bahn bunker for die-hard lovers of loud music! From drum'n'bass via noise and jungle to hardcore. *Daily 8 pm* to 4 am; Donaukanalpromenade/Augartenbrücke; U 2, U 4, Schottenring*

Jazzland [111 D1]

Dixieland, blues, boogie, swing: the venue for traditionalists. *Mon–Sat 7 pm–2 am; Franz-Josefs-Kai 29; tram: 1, 2; U 1, U 4, Schwedenplatz*

Loos-Bar [111 D4]

Place of pilgrimage for aesthetes, since the master himself, Adolf Loos, designed it. *Daily noon–4 am; Kärntner Durchgang 10; U 1, U 3, Stephansplatz*

On Broadway [111 D2–3]

Charming piano bar with plush, old Viennese ambience. Occasional evenings of political and satirical songs. *Mon–Sat 9 pm–4 am; Bauernmarkt 21; bus: 2 A, 3 A; U 1, U 2, U 3, Stephansplatz*

Planter's Club [110 C1] *Insider Tip*

🏃 Interesting bar, renovated at enormous cost, with a colonial feel to it and a huge selection of drinks. Have a meal beforehand at the Livingstone restaurant next door: exotic Californian specialities! Both *daily 5 pm–4 am; Zelinkagasse 4; tram: 1, 2; U 2, U 4, Schottenring*

Porgy & Bess [111 E4]

Central venue for jazz fans. Ambitious programme with live gigs on most days. *Mon–Fri from 9 pm, Sat&Sun from 7.30 pm; Riemergasse 11; U 3, Stubentor*

Reigen [120 B3]

🏃 Potpourri of styles, from jazz via ethnic to hardcore. Occasional discos and the odd international music star. Good food. *Daily 6 pm to 4 am; Hadikgasse 62; tram: 10, 58; U 4, Hietzing*

Szene Wien [125 D6]

Concerts from experimental to rock, generally on the hard side – punk, rock, techno or rave. *Hauffgasse 26; tram: 71*

DISCOS

🏃 Some of the discos featured here stage regular club nights and raves. You'll find times and venues in the city's listings magazines *Falter* and *City* and by phoning the *Jugend-Info (Youth Info): Tel. 17 99.*

Atrium [123 E2]

Traditional disco, various music styles. *Thurs 8.30 pm–2 am, Fri&Sat*

8.30 pm–4 am, Sun 8.30 pm–1.30 am; Schwindgasse 4; tram: D; U 1, U 2, U 4, Karlsplatz

Club Roxy [123 D2]

A little on the plush side, for 'older' disco clientele (mid-twenties onwards). Latin, funk, soul, jazz and lots of electronic sounds. *Wed–Sat 10 pm–4 am; Operngasse 24; tram: 62, 65; U 1, U 2, U 4, Karlsplatz*

Shelter [113 E6]

Small, charming cellar bar. Top-quality music from alternative to hip-hop. *Daily 8 pm–4 am; Wallensteinplatz 8; www.shelter.at; tram: 5, 33; U 4, Friedensbrücke*

Titanic [123 D1]

Two dance floors, with alternating music styles – funk, soul, rock, pop.

MARCO POLO Highlights
»Entertainment«

★ **Burgtheater**
Flagship German-language theatre (page 86)

★ **Flex**
Extra-loud, extra cool: where the in-crowd meets (page 80)

★ **Kulisse, Metropol**
Cabaret in pub-like atmosphere (page 82)

★ **Musikverein, Konzerthaus**
The height of the musical art, whether classical or modern (page 84)

★ **Odeon**
The ultimate in non-verbal performing arts (page 87)

★ **Filmmuseum**
Eldorado for film freaks (page 83)

★ **Schauspielhaus**
Exciting, uncompromising theatre – bang up-to-date (page 87))

★ **Staatsoper**
Trademark Austrian culture (page 85)

★ **Theater an der Wien**
Musicals in a charmingly plush setting (page 85)

★ **Theater in der Josefstadt**
Theatrical art for the educated classes (page 87)

Summer Stage

When the temperature rises, there's no stopping the Viennese

All summer long, it's party time on the south bank of the Danube Canal, along the Rossauer Lände **[117 E2–3]** This is where the major Viennese 'in' bars set up their outdoor 'branches' from mid-May to mid-September. There's live music, trampolining and all sorts of other outdoor activities. *Daily 3 pm–1 am; U 4, Rossauer Lände*

Good food upstairs. *Mon–Thurs 7 pm–4 am, Fri&Sat 7 pm–6 am; Theobaldgasse 11; U 2, Babenberger Strasse*

U4 [121 E5]
Classic disco: the best music from DJs who are totally in tune with latest trends. *Daily 10 pm–5 am; Schönbrunner Strasse 222; U 4, Meidlinger Hauptstrasse*

Insider Tip **Volksgarten Disco and Pavillon** [110 B4]
In-venue for people who class themselves as 'middle-aged' (in disco terms, that is, the 25- to 35-year-olds). Music: lots of experimental stuff, newest styles. The first to organise techno clubs. Ambience: plush, mirrors, plants, kidney-shaped tables. Frequent themed evenings. *Daily 11 am–2 am; Fri& Sat: club nights from 11 pm; Burggarten 1; tram: D, 1, 2, J, 46, 49; U 2, U 3, Volkstheater*

POLITICAL CABARET & MINOR STAGES

Kulisse [126 C3]
★ 🏃 Pioneer in terms of all kinds of committed cabaret, housed in an old suburban inn. Warm, welcoming pub-like atmosphere. Food and drink served during performances. *Rosensteingasse 39; Tel. 485 38 70; tram: 9, 44*

Metropol [126 C3]
★ 🏃 Like the Kulisse, typical Viennese laid-back atmosphere. Equally varied programme with more emphasis on concerts and musicals. The smaller Metropoldi and the Pawlatschenbühne in the garden are also part of the act. *Hernalser Hauptstrasse 55; Tel. 407 77 40-7; tram: 43*

Niedermair [110 A3]
🏃 Commendable cabaret stage, on which many artists began their careers and to which now famous names still like to return. *Lenaugasse 1A; Tel. 408 44 92; tram: J; U 2, Rathaus*

Original Wiener Stegreifbühne [126 C3] **Insider Tip**
A cultural curiosity: ad-lib comedy theatre. If your understanding of the dialect is up to it, a highly amusing way to spend an evening. Sausage and mustard, washed down by a beer, is an ideal accom-

paniment. *Maroltingergasse 43; Tel. 914 54 14; bus: 48 A; tram: 10, 46*

Simpl [111 E4]

Traditional stage, presenting lively, though conventional, political cabaret. *Wollzeile 36; Tel. 512 47 42-0; tram: 1, 2; U 3, Stubentor*

WUK [116 B2]

🏃 Autonomous workshop and cultural centre, the venue for music and dance, concerts, readings and exhibitions. *Währinger Strasse 59; Tel. 40 12 11-0; tram: 5, 33, 37, 38, 40–42; U 6, Volksoper*

CASINOS

Spielcasino Wien: Kärntner Strasse 41; Sun–Thurs 3 pm–3 am, Fri&Sat 3 pm–4 am; tram: D, J, 1, 2; U 1, U 2, U 4, Karlsplatz [111 D5]

How about visiting Europe's largest casino? It opened just a few years ago in Baden, 20 km south of Vienna. *Baden, spa gardens; regional train from Oper station* [126 B–C6]

Casino Wien at the Palais Esterházy

The following applies to both establishments: minimum age for visitors, 19 years of age, for players, 21 years of age. Elegant dress a must.

CINEMAS

The following cinemas specialise in original English-language films: *Burg Kino; Opernring 19; Tel. 587 84 06; www.burgkino.at; tram: D, 1, 2; U 2, Museumsquartier* [110 C5]; *Haydn Cinema. Maria-Hilfer-Strasse 57; Tel. 587 22 62; www.haydnkino.at; U 3, Neubaugasse* [122 C1]

Bellaria [110 A4] *Insider Tip*

Nostalgia for the Austria of between the wars and the post-war years. *Museumstrasse 3; Tel. 523 75 91; bus: 48 A; U 2, Volkstheater*

Filmcasino [123 D3]

International *auteur* films of recent years and retrospectives. Summer cinema in July and August. *Margaretenstrasse 78; Tel. 587 90 62; bus: 59 A; U 4, Pilgramgasse*

Filmmuseum [110 C4]

★ Mecca for cineastes shows international celluloid rarities. *Summer break: June–end of Sept; Augustinerstrasse 1; Tel. 533 70 54; tram: D, J, 1, 2; U 1, U 2, U 4, Karlsplatz*

Imax-Filmtheater [121 D3]

The cinema experience. Nature and adventure films on a 400-sq-m giant screen with six-channel sound system. *Mariahilfer Strasse 212; Info: Tel. 15 47; tram: 52, 58*

Metro Kino [111 D4]

Beautiful cinema where film buffs get together every evening to enjoy

Hit the dance floor at the Kursalon

old treasures from the Austrian film archives. *Johannesgasse 4; Tel. 512 18 03; www.filmarchiv.at; U 1, U 3, U 4, Stephansplatz*

Schikaneder Kino [123 D2]

Classic films and contemporary works make up this colourful programme. *Margaretenstrasse 24; Tel. 585 28 67; bus: 59 A; U 4, Kettenbrückengasse*

CONCERTS

Konzerthaus [111 E6]

★ This brilliant Art-Nouveau building is largely the setting for modern classics – Mahler, Bartók, Strawinsky – as well as contemporary music. All other musical genres, though, from Baroque and Renaissance down to pop and jazz, are featured on the programme. The resident orchestra at the Concert Hall – long considered a 'progressive' alternative to the more conservative Musikverein – is the Vienna Philharmonic. *Lothringerstrasse 20; Tel. 24 20 02; tram: D, 71; U 4, Stadtpark*

Kursalon [111 E5]

Maybe not perfect, but at least solidly performed; vibrant melodies in three-four time by Lanner, Strauss & Co. can be heard at this amusement pavilion on the edge of the City Park. Towards the end of each performance, the audience is invited to take to the dance floor – a rare occurrence in the waltzing capital, Vienna. *Johannesgasse 33; tickets: Tel. 512 57 90; tram: 1, 2; U 4, Stadtpark*

Musikverein [111 D6]

★ The building, commissioned by the Society of Friends of Music and built by Ringstrasse architect Theophil von Hansen from 1867 to 1869, boasts a concert hall with probably the best acoustics in the world. The magnificent Golden Hall has seen the likes of such greats of musical history as Bruckner, Mahler and Strauss down to Rubinstein, Horowitz and Karajan. To this day, this stronghold of the finest classical music tradition, welcomes the crème de la crème of international orchestras, conductors and soloists. *Bösendorferstrasse 12; Tel. 505 81 90-0; tram: D, J, 1, 2, 62, 65; U 1, U 2, U 4, Karlsplatz*

Radio-Kulturhaus [123 E2]

Innovative cultural centre at the ORF (Austrian Radio and Television) radio studios. Concerts from all musical genres take place almost daily in the main studio. An additional attraction is the 'sound theatre' Ganzohr, which takes the visitor on one-hour acoustic voyages of discovery through the world of radio. *Argentinierstrasse 30A; Ganzohr: Tues–Sun 10 am 6 pm; guided tours every hour (children must be aged 10 or over). Advance booking, info and tickets for concerts in main studio: Tel. 501 70-377; U 1, Taubstummengasse*

OPERA, OPERETTA, MUSICAL

Raimundtheater [122 A3]

For decades, the home of operettas, now mostly the venue for musicals such as *Die Schöne und das Biest* (Beauty and the Beast), *Grease* or *Das Phantom der Oper* (Phantom of the Opera). *Wallgasse 18–20; Tel. 599 77-27; tickets: Tel. 588 85; tram: 6, 18; U 6, Gumpendorfer Strasse*

Ronacher [111 D4–5]

Beautifully renovated variety theatre in the belle-époque mould. Since its re-opening some years ago, it features musicals, variety and, above all, musical guest performances. *Seilerstätte 9; Tel. 514 11-0; tickets: Tel. 588 85; tram: 1, 2; U 1, U 3, Stephansplatz*

Staatsoper [110 C5]

★ The 'Haus am Ring' symbolises like no other venue, except perhaps the Musikverein, Vienna's reputation as a music capital. Since its opening in 1869, virtually all the world's great opera singers have tread its stage, conducted by the finest conductors. As ever, between 1st September and 30th June, a different work is played almost every day. The resident orchestra is the Vienna Philharmonic.

Despite hefty state subsidies, ticket prices are high. The best seats at premieres cost up to 220 Euro. If you are prepared to go without a perfect view of the stage, you could still enjoy a splendid evening's music for around 7–20 Euro; for just 2.20 Euro you can stand in the auditorium. Admittedly you'll have to queue for a few hours at the box office ahead of the more popular performances. It's a good idea to order the desired tickets in writing in advance from the *Bundestheaterverband* (Federal Theatres Association). With luck, you could pick up an unsold, stand-by ticket from one of the ticket agencies. In an emergency, hotel porters have been known to perform small miracles where tickets are concerned! A new and highly successful addition to the Opera House is the extension on the roof terrace for children's opera! *Opernring 2; Tel. 514 44-0; tram: D, J, 1, 2, 62, 65; bus: 59 A; U 1, U 2, U 4, Karlsplatz*

Theater an der Wien [110 B6]

★ It was here, that Beethoven's *Fidelio* was heard for the first time. Opened in 1801, the theatre has seen numerous premieres of plays by Kleist, Grillparzer, Raimund and

Nestroy, plus operettas by Strauss, Suppé, Millöcker, Zeller, Lehár, Kálmán and others. Today it thrives on musical productions. During the Vienna Festival Weeks at the end of May and beginning of June, the theatre also stages high-quality drama, opera and ballet productions from home and abroad. *Linke Wienzeile 6; Tel. 588 30-0; tickets: Tel. 588 30-265; bus: 59 A; U 4, Kettenbrückengasse, U 1, U 2, U 4, Karlsplatz*

Volksoper   [116 B1]

The State Opera's 'little sister' is the place to go for light opera, lyrical drama and operetta – much of which is almost of the same high quality. *Währinger Strasse 78; Tel. 514 44-0; tram: 40–42; U 6, Währinger Strasse/Volksoper*

Insider Tip **Wiener Kammeroper**   [111 E3]

The Chamber Opera is known for its fresh, unconventional productions featuring little-known voices.

In the summer, the ensemble transfers to Schloss Schönbrunn, where it entertains visitors with opera and operetta in the Palace Theatre. *Fleischmarkt 24; Tel. 512 01 00-77; bus: 2 A; U 4, Schwedenplatz; Schönbrunn Palace Theatre; Tel. 877 45 66; tram: 58; U 4, Schönbrunn*

THEATRE

Akademietheater   [111 E6]

This annexe of the Burgtheater, with which it shares an ensemble, specialises in 20th-century classics and contemporary drama. *Lisztstrasse 1; Tel. 514 44-41 40; tram: D, 71; U 4, Stadtpark*

Burgtheater   [110 B3]

★ Flagship of German-language drama. Scene of many stormy, yet refreshing confrontations during the directorship of Claus Peymann (1989–99) between the theatre director, parts of the ensemble, the

The Burgtheater: a splendid backdrop for exciting performances

press and the more conservative elements of its audience. As ever, guaranteed to produce the highest quality classical and contemporary drama. *Dr.-Karl-Lueger-Ring 2; Tel. 514 44-0; tram: D, 1, 2; U 3, Herrengasse*

Gruppe 80 [122 B2]
Medium-sized theatre with often unconventional performances. The company specialises in new takes on the classics. *Gumpendorfer Strasse 67; Tel. 586 52 22-0; bus: 13 A, 57 A; U 4, Pilgramgasse*

International Theatre [117 D2]
Small, but impressive English-language theatre featuring up-market light comedy to classical drama. *Porzellangasse 8/Müllnergasse 6A; Tel. 319 62 72; tram: D; bus: 40 A*

Vienna's English Theatre [116 C4-C5]
The repertoire of Europe's oldest foreign-language theatre, founded in 1963, reaches from Shakespere via thrillers to farce. *Josefsgasse 12; Tel 402 12 60; tram: J, 1, 2, D; bus: 13 A; U 2, Rathaus, U 3, Volkstheater*

Odeon [111 E2]
★ Erwin Piplit's Serapionstheater has made an excellent international reputation for itself with its unusual performances, a mixture of acting, pantomime, dance and music. Frequent guest performances by like-minded ensembles. *Taborstrasse 10; Tel. 214 55 62-20; tram: 1, 2, 21, N*

Schauspielhaus [117 D2]
★ Under the committed directorship of Hans Gratzer, the theatre has managed to defend its reputation as the city's leading avant-garde stage. Exciting opera productions are a recent addition to its repertoire. *Porzellangasse 19; Tel. 317 01 01; tram: D*

Theater in der Josefstadt [116 B4]
★ Guardian of sophisticated conversation pieces and light comedy, with occasional forays into the world of sublime classical theatre and dramatic contemporary literature. The theatre has recently shown a leaning towards innovative material and performances, which do not always meet with the unconditional approval of its traditionally conservative audience. *Josefstädter Strasse 26; Tel. 427 00-300; www.josefstadt.org; tram: J; bus: 13 A*

Theater am Schwedenplatz [111 E2]
For decades now, inspired solo entertainer Herbert Lederer has been tirelessly writing his own consistently high-quality, literary text collages, which he then performs in this one-man basement theatre. In the summer months he performs his programme on a farm in the Salzburg region. *Franz-Josefs-Kai 21; Tel. 535 79 14; tram: 1, 2; U 1, U 4, Schwedenplatz*

Die Theater Wien
Union of two small theatres, specialising in anything on a scale from exciting avant-garde to second-class minority-interest features. *Konzerthaus Lothringerstrasse 20 [111 E6]; Künstlerhaus Karlsplatz 5 [111 D6]; both Tel. 587 05 04-0; U 1, U 2, U 4, Karlsplatz*

Emperors, churches, coffee houses

These walking tours are marked in green on the map on the back cover and in the Street Atlas beginning on page 110

1 BACK IN TIME TO THE MIDDLE AGES

This tour through the historical heart of the city takes you from St. Stephen's Cathedral through picturesque winding streets and courtyards, past the oldest churches and Roman foundations into the former Jewish Quarter. Allow half a day for the tour, if you want to see the most important sights from the inside too and maybe still have time for a coffee break.

Set off at Vienna's holiest spot and probably most famous landmark – the *Stephansdom (p. 33)*, whose 850th anniversary was celebrated with great pomp by the Viennese in 1997. Having duly admired this filigree sandstone masterpiece inside and out, and possibly also having climbed the tower, it's just a few steps from its southeastern corner to Singerstrasse. Here, at No.7, keen art lovers should visit the *Schatzkammer des Deutschen Ordens (p. 48)*.

The idle pleasures of the Burggarten – very inviting!

Right on the next corner, turn left into *Blutgasse* – a prime example of urban redevelopment, featuring cobbled streets, ancient buildings and several sleepy courtyards ringed by long wooden balconies, so-called 'Pawlatschen'. At the end of the narrow street stands the *Figaro-Haus (p. 48)*, in which Wolfgang Amadeus Mozart lived from 1784 to 1787 and where he wrote, among other things, the opera of the same name.

Continue along narrow side streets via Schulerstrasse and Wollzeile into bustling *Bäckerstrasse*, which is lined with famous-name fashionable bars, such as the Neu Wien restaurant or the VIP pub Oswald & Kalb. Carry on heading east towards *Dr.-Ignaz-Seipel-Platz*, one of the most impressive squares in the city, which is spectacularly illuminated every evening. The early Baroque façade on the north side belongs to the *Universitätskirche* (University Church). Behind this, to the left, in the Great Hall of the Old University is the seat of Austria's *Akademie der Wissenschaften (p. 22)*.

It's just a short way along Sonnenfelsgasse, then you turn right

Insider Tip

The Vienna Synagogue in Seitenstettengasse

into the astonishingly crooked *Schönlaterngasse*. Here, at No. 7, a carving in the sandstone façade symbolises the well-known 13th-century legend of the mythical basilisk, a deadly serpent which was said to have lived in the well in the rear courtyard and terrorised the inhabitants. Directly next door is a passageway leading to *Heiligen-kreuzer Hof (p. 38)*, a large and particularly idyllic courtyard.

Leaving this via the gateway opposite, you then turn right twice and come shortly afterwards to Vienna's oldest restaurant: the *Griechenbeisl (p. 55)* was established over 500 years ago and can still be recommended today. The vaulted ceiling of one of its rooms bears the original signatures of dozens of historical and literary greats, including Wolfgang Amadeus Mozart, Ludwig van Beethoven and Albert Einstein.

Following the Fleischmarkt to the west and crossing Rotenturm-strasse, you come to the so-called *Bermudadreieck*, a lively bar and pub quarter. Among the pioneers of the scene here are the still-trendy *Salzamt* restaurant, the *Roter Engel* bar and the *Krah-Krah (p. 59)*, a Mecca for beer fans. In the midst of all this, is one of the city's oldest churches, the Romanesque *Rup-rechtskirche (p. 33)*, an oasis of peace in this bustling corner of the city. A little off the beaten track in Seitenstettengasse is the *Stadt-tempel der Israelitischen Kultus-gemeinde* (Vienna Synagogue). It is the work of the Classicist architect Josef Kornhäusel, and is the only one of Vienna's original 24 syna-gogues to survive the pogrom of November, 1938.

The next stage of your city tour takes you along Judengasse – with its numerous boutiques, a must for fashion freaks – as far as the *Hoher Markt (p. 38)*. Take the chance to go down and look at the foun-dations of the Roman settlement

Vindobona. In the eastern corner of the square is the *Anchor Clock*, whose Art-Nouveau figures parade to the sound of organ music across the face of the clock every day at noon. After a detour via Salvatorgasse to the *Maria am Gestade church (p. 32)*, a little-heeded Gothic gem, you come past two magnificent Baroque buildings, the former *Böhmische Hofkanzlei* (Bohemian Court Chancellery) and the *Altes Rathaus* (Old Town Hall).

Via Judenplatz and the new Holocaust Memorial head along Drahtgasse you arrive at the so-called *Hof* (courtyard). This astonishingly spacious square, on which the Babenberg Duke Heinrich II once had the Vienna Residence built, is lined with a number of splendid façades. Its most attractive feature is the *Kirche am Hof (p. 32)*, on the eastern side. From its balcony, Emperor Franz II proclaimed the end of the Holy Roman Empire in 1806.

2 ON THE EMPEROR'S TRACKS: THE HOFBURG AND ITS ENVIRONS

A wander through the labyrinth of the former Habsburg Residence takes you to their Treasure Chamber, their last resting places, the Lipizzaner horses, diverse unique museums and probably the most beautiful library in the world. Despite the short total distance, we recommend allowing at least three hours for this imperial tour.

Starting point of the tour is the *Staatsoper (p. 30)* or, to be precise, the square to its rear, *Albertina-platz*. Here, not far from the Hotel Sacher, the *Mahnmal gegen Krieg (p. 20)*, a memorable group of sculptures created by Alfred Hrdlicka, commemorates the victims of National Socialism. Here, too, stands the *Albertina (p. 42)*, the former palace of Albert, Duke of Sachsen-Teschen, which has recently been re-opened and contains the largest collection of graphic art in the world – around 1.5 million prints. Diagonally opposite is another star of every sightseeing agenda, the world's largest *Theatermuseum (p. 47)*, housed in Palais Lobkowitz.

Our route now leads along Augustinerstrasse to *Josefsplatz (p. 38)*, thanks to its stylistic unity, a stunningly beautiful Baroque ensemble. Immediately to the left is the main entrance of the *Augustinerkirche (p. 30)*, parish church of the imperial court, in which the Habsburgs celebrated their weddings and kept preserved the hearts of their ancestors. The long side of the square is taken up by the Great Hall of the *Österreichische Nationalbibliothek*, belonging to the *Hofburg (p. 24)*, a grandiose creation by Baroque architect Fischer von Erlach and his son, and something which is strongly recommended visiting. Another 'must see' is a performance by the Lipizzaner horses in the neighbouring *Winterreitschule* (Winter Riding School). These legendary white horses are kept around the corner in the *Stallburg* (stables). Its fine arcades make this Vienna's most significant Renaissance building.

Stroll under the arcades and the narrow Reitschulgasse until you reach *Michaelerplatz*. In the centre, archaeologists have recently dis-

the remains of a Roman [...]. On the northern side stands the *Looshaus (p. 26)*. Created shortly before World War I by Adolf Loos, its stark, unadorned façade came in for harsh criticism at the time, but is now seen as a milestone of modern architecture. Only a few years ago, a local bank had this symbol of an entire era painstakingly restored, down to the very last detail. Visitors have since been even more enthusiastic about the simple elegance of the marble façade and wood-panelled foyer.

Those of you who suddenly feel the need to do some shopping are advised to make a detour at this stage and pop over to the neighbouring *Kohlmarkt*, one of Vienna's most elegant – and naturally enough most expensive – shopping streets. Not so long ago, a number of glamorous and internationally-famous fashion houses, among them Prada, Gucci and Louis Vuitton, set up branches alongside the old established shops, pushing prices up still further. If you'd rather take a break over coffee and cake, look no further than *Griensteidl* at *Michaelerplatz 2*, or, a few steps further on at *Demel* at *Kohlmarkt 14*. Both establishments are rightly considered to be classics on the Viennese coffee-house scene. Demel not only sells world-famous delicacies for the sweet-toothed, but also regularly delights passers-by with its window decorations consisting of exquisitely decorated groups of figures made of icing sugar.

Back on course, the route now brings you to the *Hofburg (p. 24)*, to be precise, through St. Michael's Gate – overlooked by a massive copper dome turned green with age

Lipizzaner parade at the Spanische Hofreitschule

– and into the Inner Courtyard. To the right, in the so-called Imperial Chancellery Wing, is the entrance to the *Kaiserappartements (p. 43)*, the studies and private rooms of Emperor Franz Joseph and his beloved Elisabeth. The same entrance leads to the Imperial Silver Collection, equally worth seeing. Leave the southeast corner of the square through the shopping arcade; soon afterwards you are standing on *Heldenplatz (p. 38)*. Take a deep breath. Here, on this gigantic open space, you are enveloped by the entire feudal splendour of the huge former Habsburg empire. In front of you are the outlines of some of the most famous Ringstrasse buildings. To the north-west stands the *Parlament (p. 27)*, behind it the *Rathaus (p. 26)*, immediately to the left of the parliament building is the *Justizpalast* (Palace of Justice). To the south-west, the *Naturhistorisches Museum (p. 46)* and the *Kunsthistorisches Museum (p. 44)* stand behind the fortress-like Outer Castle Gate, which was originally built to commemorate the battle against Napoleon at Leipzig. Behind you is the Leopoldine Wing, which today is the official residence of the Austrian President.

Finally, the mighty semi-circular building to the east is the *Neue Hofburg* (New Palace). It contains several highly interesting museums, such as the *Museum für Völkerkunde (p. 45)*, the Ephesus Museum, plus the Collections of Arms and Armour and of Ancient Musical Instruments (both sections of the Museum of Fine Arts). The left wing of the New Palace houses the Congress Centre, a conference venue which is hard to beat, in terms of luxury and ambience. The apartments of Empress Maria Theresia and Field Marshal Radetzky, plus the Marble and Metternich Rooms, Ceremonial Hall and Grand Ballroom, where grandiose Baroque operas were premiered in the 18th century and where Emperor Joseph II's wedding breakfast took place ... And so it goes on; in an area of over 11,000 sq m, decorated with the most sumptuous ornamental plasterwork and equipped with the latest communications technology, these facilities underline Vienna's reputation as a world-wide centre for international diplomacy.

Return, though, to the Inner Courtyard and turn to the right through the Renaissance gateway adorned with coats of arms. Through here you enter the oldest part of the castle complex, the Swiss Courtyard, first documented as early as the end of the 13th century. From here, it is essential that you visit the *Schatzkammer (p. 48)*. It contains the world's most important collection of its kind – almost intact set of medieval crown jewels, namely the imperial regalia of the Holy Roman Empire of the German Nation. In addition, it houses the treasures of Burgundy and the Order of the Golden Fleece and also the inalienable Habsburg heirlooms. Hidden away in an adjoining courtyard stands the Palace Chapel, an architectural gem of the Gothic era, in which the Vienna Choirboys sing religious works by Mozart, Haydn or Schubert on Sundays and public holidays – an unforgettable experience *(order tickets in writing a few weeks in advance from the Hofmusikkapelle, Hofburg, 1010 Vienna)*.

A fitting, if somewhat morbid, conclusion to this tour is a visit to the *Kaisergruft (p. 21)* underneath the Capuchin Church on the Neuer Markt. Here, 145 members of the Habsburg family lie buried, some in highly decorative sarcophagi, including Empress Maria Theresia and her husband Franz Stephan, Joseph II, Franz Joseph and his wife Sisi and son Rudolph. You can reach this venerable resting place by crossing Josefplatz and following Augustinerstrasse back to Albertinaplatz. From here, turn left down Tegetthoffstrasse as far as the Neuer Markt.

Monasteries, vineyards and expansive forests

Hills right on the doorstep; Laxenburg; along the Wine Route to Baden; in the Vienna Woods; to the Marchfeld

KAHLENBERG AND LEOPOLDSBERG

[126–127 C–D2] **Both hills are right on Vienna's doorstep and can be reached easily, with the 38 A bus from the U-Bahn station Heiligenstadt (U 4, U 6), coming by car from the city centre, you drive via Grinzing. Those who enjoy walking can follow the Schreiberbach through the Mukental (valley), finally climbing a long flight of steps onto the Kahlenberg and then on to the Leopoldsberg. The walk takes around two hours.**

This outing is worth making for the fabulous panoramic view of Vienna and the entire basin in which the city lies, as far as the Leitha mountains and the Slovakian Carpathian range – weather conditions and visibility permitting.

The Donauauen are a paradise not only for canoeists

Both 'peaks' in the northwest of the city are not only the natural elevations which lie furthest to the northeast in the Vienna Woods, but also in the entire Alpine range. Until the late 18th century, the 484-m-high Kahlenberg had been known as the 'Sauberg' (pig's hill) because of the large numbers of wild boar which roamed its dense woodland. At that time, the neighbouring hilltop, 60 m lower down, bore the name 'Kahlenberg'. When a church was built here in 1683 in honour of the reigning Emperor Leopold I, the ground it stood upon was given the illustrious imperial name instead. The Sauberg was duly re-christened Kahlenberg.

Amongst the ruins of a 13th-century Babenberg fortress on Leopoldsberg stands the tiny St. Leopold's Church with its characteristic twin-tower façade. A good place to stop for a bite to eat – plus a view of Vienna – is the *Restaurant Burg Leopoldsberg; Tel. 370 16 80;* summer: Mon–Sat 11 am–11 pm, Sun until 8 pm; winter: daily 11 am to 6 pm; €€. Its culinary counter-

Insider Tip

95

part lies right next to the St. Joseph's Church and offers its guests a similarly fantastic view: the *Landgasthof Kahlenberg; open all year round; daily;* €€. Suitably refreshed in body and mind, you could now set off – by bus or by car – on a trip along the 'Höhenstrasse' a panoramic route through the Vienna Woods, laid out in the 1930s as job-creation project. Roads branch off into the Heuriger districts Sievering, Neustift, Pötzleinsdorf and Salmannsdorf.

LAINZER TIERGARTEN

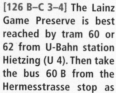

[126 B–C 3–4] The Lainz Game Preserve is best reached by tram 60 or 62 from U-Bahn station Hietzing (U 4). Then take the bus 60 B from the Hermesstrasse stop as far as Lainzer Tor.

Vienna's above-average quality of life is due to its green belt. The Vienna Woods, immortalised in songs, poems and waltz melodies, and covering some 1,250 sq km, partly enclose the west of the city. Some 25 sq km of this area, the so-called Lainz Game Preserve, lies within the city boundary. The Viennese use this last untouched section of the Vienna Woods for recreation purposes. An 80-km-long network of signposted footpaths and numerous places to stop for a snack mean this is an ideal place for long walks – and frequent breaks!

In the Middle Ages, the woods served the Babenberg family as a private game preserve. In 1782, Emperor Joseph II had the 'Royal Hunting Grounds' enclosed by a 24-km-long stone wall, which still stands today. The park was only made accessible to the general public in 1919.

There's a fine view of the woodland round about from the top of the ◀▶ *Hubertuswarte*. The park's biggest attraction, however, is the *Hermesvilla* which is situated close to the Lainzer Tor. This Historicist hunting lodge was built between 1882 and 1886 by Ringstrasse architect Karl von Hasenauer as a gift from Emperor Franz Joseph to his beloved Elisabeth. Now an annexe of the Historical Museum of the City of Vienna, it is regularly used to hold interesting exhibitions.

Two tips for a break and a bite to eat: the tourist café *Zum Hirschg'stemm (approx. 1 hour's walk from the Lainzer Tor; no Tel.; mid-Feb to mid-Nov: daily 10 am–6 pm at the latest;* €*)* and the café-restaurant *Hermesvilla; Tel. 804 13 23; Tues to Sun 9 am–6 pm; winter: until approx. 4.30 pm only;* €.

LAXENBURG

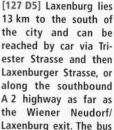

[127 D5] Laxenburg lies 13 km to the south of the city and can be reached by car via Triester Strasse and then Laxenburger Strasse, or along the southbound A 2 highway as far as the Wiener Neudorf/ Laxenburg exit. The bus to Eisenstadt (every hour from Wien Mitte) also stops in Laxenburg.

The castle complex at Laxenburg is very pretty, but prettier still is its magnificent, approximately 2.5-sq-km park. It features several ponds and is criss-crossed by canals

The Middle Ages as the Biedermeier ideal: the Franzensburg in Laxenburg

– ideal for a boat trip in summer or for ice-skating in winter.

As early as the 14th century, the Habsburgs owned a small hunting lodge here, in the midst of the water meadows. The lodge was largely destroyed in 1683 during the second Turkish attack on Vienna, and was later replaced by a larger one under Leopold I. Empress Maria Theresia then had a late-Baroque summer residence, the 'Blauer Hof' (Blue Court), built for her 18-member family. Emperor Franz Joseph I spent part of his childhood here and Crown Prince Rudolf was born here.

As you walk along the extensive network of pathways, lined by imposing old trees, you come across follies, mock Greek temples, neo-Gothic bridges, pavilions, monuments and grottoes. The most impressive architectural proof of the Habsburg's obsession with history is the Franzensburg, built between 1798 and 1836. Emperor Franz I (II) had this 'garden house

in the guise of a fortified castle' built in the spirit of the narrow-minded, ultra-German Biedermeier era. It stands on an island in the middle of a huge pond and is furnished with countless treasures which the Emperor, in an attempt to capture best the ideal of a medieval stronghold, had confiscated in castles, churches and monasteries from all over his realm.

The walk from the entrance to the park to the ferry boats, with which you can cross to the pseudo castle, takes roughly half an hour. The park is open all year round. *Guided tours of the Franzensburg: Easter–Oct: in fine weather daily (according to demand) 11 am, 2 pm and 3 pm.* **Insider Tip**

There are a number of nice places to stop for refreshments: on the Franzensburg island, the *Café-Meierei (Tel. 02236-713 75; Apr to Oct: daily 10 am–6 pm; Nov–Mar: daily until 5 pm only; €€),* and in front of the park entrance, on the right on the Schlossplatz, the

Laxenburger Hof (Tel. 02236-723 76; Tues–Sun 9 am–10 pm; €€).

HEILIGENKREUZ AND MAYERLING

[126 A–B 5–6] The Heiligenkreuz Monastery lies approx. 30 km from Vienna and can be reached by car via the southbound A 2 highway as far as the intersection at Vösendorf, and from there along the A 21 bypass as far as the Heiligenkreuz exit. The quickest route by public transport is by S-Bahn (suburban railway, lines 1 and 2), by train from the Südbahnhof or with the regional train from Wien-Staatsoper to Baden and from there with the mail bus.

Although little of the original medieval monastery complex at Heiligenkreuz remains intact, it is nevertheless truly impressive. There is, for example, a magnificent partly Romanesque, partly Gothic collegiate church, with altarpieces by Michael Rottmayr and splendidly carved choir stalls. Further highlights are close at hand; the marvellous cloisters with 13th-century glass windows, a pump room and finally a chapterhouse containing the graves of early Babenberg rulers.

Heiligenkreuz is the oldest Cistercian monastery in Austria and was founded by Margrave Leopold III in 1133. It soon developed into the cultural centre of the southern Vienna Woods *(daily 9 am–11.30 am, 1.45 pm–5 pm; winter: until 4 pm; guided tours: daily 10 am,* 11 am, 2 pm, 3 pm and 4 pm, Sun *from 11 am).*

Just 5 km to the west is Mayerling, a place shrouded in legend. The hunting lodge in which the Habsburg Crown Prince Rudolf and his mistress Baroness Mary Vetsera committed suicide in 1889 was subsequently transformed into a Carmelite convent. Visitors to the affiliated church are also shown a collection of mementoes relating to the tragic couple *(daily 9 am to 12.30 pm, 1.30 pm–5 pm, Sun from 10 am).*

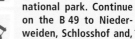

MARCHFELD CASTLES AND DANUBE WATER MEADOWS

[127 F 3–4] and further east By car, take the primary route No. 3 from the Stadlau intersection via Gross-Enzersdorf to Orth, Eckartsau and the national park. Continue on the B 49 to Niederweiden, Schlosshof and, a good 10 km to the north, to Marchegg. Without a car, the journey is difficult. Four times a day, a mail bus runs from Vienna–Orth–Eckartsau–Stopfenreuth–Hainburg (from Wien Mitte; journey time: over 2 hours). From Wien Mitte or Nord you can take the S 1 to Gänserndorf and from there the regional train to Marchegg. Neither Schlosshof nor Niederweiden can be reached by bus or rail. Visitors to the national park should remember to pack an insect repellent in summer!

The *Marchfeld,* the flat expanse of border country to the east of Vienna, between the rivers Danube and March, is today the city's chief

Seemingly unapproachable, yet open to the public: Schloss Marchegg

grain and vegetable supplier. In the past, these were favourite hunting grounds with the nobility, who built a series of magnificent hunting lodges, the finest of which can be visited on a day trip along the 'Marchfeld Castle Route', starting in Vienna.

The most interesting of these noblemen's houses are the *Schlosshof,* whose Baroque exterior as we see it today was designed by Lukas von Hildebrandt at the request of Prince Eugene; then there is the neighbouring *Schloss Niederweiden,* considerably more delicate in style, by Johann Bernhard Fischer von Erlach; the Baroque *Schloss Marchegg,* which contains an interesting hunting museum; *Schloss Orth,* which has a medieval feel to it, featuring high hipped roofs and four mighty corner towers; and finally the hunting lodge in *Eckartsau,* re-designed in the Baroque style by Joseph Emanuel Fischer von Erlach and set in a delightful park.

A visit to the *Donauauen* (Danube water meadows) near Stopfenreuth/Hainburg is sure to be an unforgettable experience. This over 90-sq-km expanse of Central-European primeval forest was turned into a national park in 1996 and can be explored on foot, in a horse-drawn carriage or in a canoe *(Information and registration for guided tours: Apr–beginning Nov: Tel. 02214-22 32).*

Insider Tip

99

Absolutely in!

Essential events, meetings and happenings you can't afford to miss

Dance floor day in, day out

The Babenberger Passage, a subway at the lower end of Mariahilfer Strasse, at the junction of Babenberger Strasse and Burgring, is turning into the city's newest and most happening dance venue. All year round, day in, day out, bop till you drop to the early hours – to the hottest sounds, mixed by top-flight DJs (*www.sunshine.at*).

Club Schikaneder

In the middle of the latest scene district, the Freihaus Quarter, a formerly rather conservative arts cinema has been transformed into a multimedia, extremely smart art and dance location. Alongside cinematic delicacies (3 to 5 films a day, also at midnight), the Club Schikaneder also serves up daily readings, exhibitions and first-class DJ-lines to groove to. *Margaretenstrasse 24; Tel. 585 28 67 (cinema); www.schikaneder.at*

Friday night skating

Between May and September the Vienna's Green Party organises a huge skating event every Friday. 'Quer durch die Nacht, quer durch die Stadt' (Through the night, through the city) is the motto of this 80-minute tour covering around 12 km of streets normally the domain of motorised traffic. Fee: none; routes: variable; start: *10 pm on Heldenplatz; www.wien.gruene.at*

Climbing the 'Flakturm'

Vienna goes Alpine! Scale the heights of the former anti-aircraft tower in Esterházy Park. Degree of difficulty: 4–8; height: up to 34 m; 3,000 grips; 15 routes. *Apr–Oct: Mon–Fri from 2 pm, Sat&Sun and publ. hols 1 pm until dusk; Info hotline: Tel. 585 47 48; www.oeav-events.at/flakturm*

On the trail of the Third Man

Through the city and down into the Vienna underworld. Experience at first hand the return of the legendary film character portrayed by Orson Welles. Don't forget to wear flat shoes and warm clothing. Bring a torch – and strong nerves! *Mon&Fri 4 pm; approx. 2.5 hours; 16 Euro; Tel. 774 89 01*

From banks to time zones

Useful addresses and information for your trip to Vienna

CURRENCY BANKS & CREDIT CARDS

Legal tender in Austria is the Euro. One Euro = 100 cents. Bank notes to the value of 5, 10, 20, 50, 100, 200 and 500 Euro and coins to the value of 1, 2, 5, 10, 20 and 50 cents and 1 and 2 Euro are in circulation. Bank opening times are as follows: *Mon—Wed&Fri 8 am to 3 pm, Thurs 8 am–5.30 pm; smaller branches close for lunch from 12.30 pm–1.30 pm.* Cash dispensers are plentiful. Most major credit cards are accepted everywhere without any problems. If you lose your card, notify your credit card company immediately under the following numbers: *American Express: Tel. 515 11-0; Diners Club: Tel. 501 35-0; Eurocard: Tel. 717 01-0; Visa: Tel. 711 11-770*

CUSTOMS

Travellers from other EU countries are no longer subject to customs checks. The following limits apply to goods brought into Austria: goods for personal use up to the value of 175 Euro, 800 cigarettes, 400 cigarillos, 200 cigars, 1 kg tobacco, plus 10 l spirits, 90 l wine and 110 l beer. Non-EU citizens can bring the following items into Austria: 200 cigarettes, 100 cigarillos, 50 cigars, 250 g tobacco, plus 1 l spirits, 2 l wine.

DRIVING

EU drivers must hold a valid driving licence. In addition, drivers from outside the EU require an IDP (International Driving Permit), obtainable from automobile clubs at home. Drivers and passengers must wear a seat belt at all times; motorcyclists must wear a helmet. The maximum level of alcohol in the blood is 0.5 mg/l. The use of cellphones while driving is prohibited, except with hands-free systems. Speed limits are as follows: on highways: 130 km/h (80 mph), overland: 100 km/h (62 mph), in built-up areas: 50 km/h (30 mph). Both of Austria's automobile clubs offer an emergency 24-hr breakdown service (fee for non-members): *ÖAMTC: Tel. 120; ARBÖ: Tel. 123.*

Austria's highways are subject to a toll, so you must purchase a vignette. These are available at border crossings, filling stations and tobacconist's and cost, for example, 7.60 Euro for ten days. Parking during the daytime in the inner districts of Vienna is subject to charge. There are several large car parks in the city centre. Ask at your hotel for a special hotel parking ticket, or for tips as to where you can find an alternative, cheap parking space.

EMBASSIES

UK Embassy [124 A2]
1030 Vienna, Jauresgasse 10–12; Tel. 716 13-0; tram: 71; bus: 4 A; U 4, Stadtpark

US Embassy [116 C2]
1090 Vienna, Boltzmanngasse 16; Tel. 313 39-0; tram: 37, 38, 40 A; U 6, Währinger Strasse/Volksoper

Canadian Embassy [117 F4]
1010 Vienna, Laurenzerberg 2; Tel. 531 38 30 00; tram: 1, 2, 21, N; bus: 2 A; U 1, U 4, Schwedenplatz

EMERGENCIES

Fire brigade: *Tel. 122;* Police: *Tel. 133;* Ambulance: *Tel. 144;* Emergency doctor: *Tel. 531 16-0;* 24-hr pharmacy: *Tel. 15 50;* Emergency dental service: *Tel. 512 20 78*

FIACRE

The cost of this particular pleasure trip is pretty steep, depending on the number of passengers. Agree the fare before setting off. A 90-minute tour costs around 95 Euro; the 20-minute version will set you back 40 Euro. Fiacre ranks are in Augustinerstrasse in front of the Albertina [130 C4], on Heldenplatz between the two equestrian statues [130 B4] and on Stephansplatz at the northern end of the cathedral [131 D3].

GETTING TO VIENNA

By air

The international airport lies approx. 15 km southeast of the city centre in Schwechat. Austrian Airlines and other major carriers fly direct from all major European cities. Austrian Airlines also flies direct from New York and Washington and from Montreal and Toronto *(www.vienna airport.com; www.aua.com).* A bus service links the City Air Terminal and the Südbahnhof and Westbahnhof in the city. Journey time: 20–30 mins., single ticket: 5.80 Euro. Alternatively you can take the train to Wien Mitte station. Single ticket: 3 Euro. A taxi ride into the city will cost approx. 35 Euro.

By train

International train services arriving via Germany and Switzerland terminate at the Westbahnhof, a major intersection of several U-Bahn, tram, S-Bahn (suburban trains) and regional lines. From London there are two main train routes to Vienna: via Paris – with Eurostar and Euronight – or via Lille, Brussels, Frankfurt and Nuremberg. *www.oebb.at*

By car

Vienna is well served by the major European highway network. From London, drive to Vienna via Brussels, Stuttgart, Munich (all toll-free highways) and Salzburg. Don't forget to buy a vignette (see 'Driving').

By bus

The European express coach company Eurolines has a rapidly expanding network of routes which includes Vienna. The London to Vienna service runs daily, except

Mondays and Thursdays. *www. eurolines.com*

HEALTH

In the event of sickness, pay doctor's bills and prescription charges immediately and claim back your costs on your return home. Visitors from Britain should have the E111 form with them. Visitors from the US and Canada should make sure their health insurance covers foreign travel and, if necessary, take out extra insurance for the duration of their holiday.

INFORMATION IN VIENNA

Vienna Tourist Board   [110 C5]
General information, what's on and where to stay. *Tourist Info Vienna: 1025 Vienna, Albertinaplatz (on the corner with Maysederstrasse); daily 9 am–7 pm; Tel. 01-245 55; Fax 245 55-666; www.wien.info; info @info.wien.at. Also in the arrivals hall at the airport; daily 8.30 am to 9 pm*

Wien Xtra Jugend-Info   [110 B5]
Tickets and information with the under-26 age group in mind. *Mon–Sat noon–7 pm; 1010 Vienna, Babenbergerstrasse (on the corner with Burgring); Tel. 01-17 99; www. jugendinfowien.at; jugendinfowien @wienXtra.at*

INTERNET

In addition to the websites listed above and under 'Pre-Travel Information', there are a number of other interesting sites. *www.wien.gv.at:* official city website. *www.falter.at:* online city listings magazine *(German only). Current exhibitions at Austria's state-run museums: www. nhm-wien.ac.at/bundesmuseen;*

www.marcopolo.de

Web travel news plus insider tips

MARCO POLO is also on the internet, with information on over 4,000 destinations. Are you heading for Paris, the Dominican Republic or the Australian outback? Just a mouse-click away, at www.marcopolo.de, you'll find all you need to know about your desired location. In addition to travel guide information, the website also contains:

• up-to-the-minute travel news and interesting reports
• regular special features and competitions
• mini guides to print out yourself

You can help us: Tell us your own personal insider tip and find out about other MARCO POLO readers' experiences at your chosen destination. Collect your favourite tips in your MARCO POLO diary. The world at your fingertips at www.marcopolo.de! Get all the latest information and make more out of your travels!

(links to Vienna's main museums, most of which have an English version). Visit *www.hofburg-wien.at* or *www.schoenbrunn.at* to whet your appetite. *www.virtualvienna.net:* English site dedicated to ex-pat residents, but with lots of information to interest visitors too.

INTERNET CAFÉS

rhiz [116 A4]

Chat in trendy, arty ambience. *Mon–Sat 6 pm–4 am, Sun 6 pm to 2 am; Lerchenfelder Gürtel, U-Bahn archways 37–38; Tel. 409 25 05; U 6, Josefstädter Strasse*

Bignet I & II [111 D3, D5]

The whole world of modern communication – here you can chat, scan, print and burn CDs. Cheap telephone rates, too. *Daily 10 am to midnight; Hoher Markt 8–9; Tel. 533 29 39; U 1, U 3, Stephansplatz; Kärntner Strasse 61; Tel. 503 98 44; U 1, U 2, U 4, Karlsplatz*

LOST PROPERTY

Main lost property office: *Mon to Wed&Fri 8 am–3.30 pm, Thurs 8 am to 5.30 pm.* Processing of claims by telephone or online only, *Tel. 40 00-80 91;* outside office hours, under the hotline *Tel. 0900-60 02 00* (liable to charge) or via the internet: *www.fundamt.gv.at*

PASSPORT & VISA

Visas are not required for EU citizens; citizens of the USA or Canada require a visa only if staying for longer than three months. A valid identity card or passport is sufficient to allow entry into Austria.

POST

Post offices open generally as follows: *Mon–Fri 8 am–noon, 2 pm to 6 pm;* district post offices: *Mon–Fri 7 am–7 pm, Sat 7 am–10 am;* main post office [111 E3]: *daily 24-hrs; Fleischmarkt 19; U 4, Schwedenplatz.* Stamps are also available from tobacconist's.

PRE-TRAVEL INFORMATION

Austrian National Tourist Office
UK: *P.O. Box 2363; London W1A 2QB; Tel. 020 7629 0461; Fax 020 7499 6038; www.austria-tourism.at/uk*

USA: *Travel Information Center; P.O. Box 1142; New York; NY 10018; Tel. 212 944 6880; Fax 212 736 4568; www.austria-tourism.at/us*

Canada: *Travel Information Center; 2, Bloor Street East – Suite 3330; Toronto M4W 1A8; Tel. 416 967 3381; Fax 416 967 4101; www.austria-tourism.at/us*

PUBLIC TRANSPORT

Vienna's public transport network comprises five U-Bahn (underground train) lines, several S-Bahn (suburban train) lines and numerous tram, bus and night bus services. Tickets are available from tobacconist's and from the ticket machines at U-Bahn stations; night bus tickets must be bought from the driver. Single ticket: 1.50 Euro; day ticket: 5 Euro; 8-day strip ticket: 24 Euro (can be used by several people at once – just stamp a strip for each person per day). *www.wienerlinien.at*

SIGHTSEEING TOURS

On rails: the Oldtimer Tram along Ringstrasse and into the Prater. *May–Oct: Sat 11.30 am and 1.30 pm, Sun and publ. hols also 9.30 am; Tel. 79 09-440 26. Departure point: Karlsplatz/Otto-Wagner-Pavillon; duration: approx. 1 hr; 15 Euro*

By bicycle: Guided bike tours (2–3 hrs) by *Bike & Guide; 1020 Vienna, Rueppgasse 2–9* **[118 B2]***; Tel./Fax 212 11 35;* and by *Pedal Power; 1020 Vienna, Ausstellungsstrasse 3* **[118 C3]***; Tel./Fax 729 72 34*

By bus: Several tours daily: *Vienna Sightseeing Tours; Tel. 712 46 83 0;* and *Cityrama; Tel. 534 13 0. Vienna Line Hop On Hop Off* buses: daily 8 am–6 pm every hour (Fri to Sun every half-hour); three fixed routes covering 13 stops. With a two-day ticket for 20 Euro (children: 7 Euro) you can hop on and hop off as you please. Main stop: in front of the Staatsoper. Information: hotels and travel agencies. Alternative bus or bike tours on special themes, e.g. 'Art Nouveau' and 'Red Vienna': *Stattwerkstatt; 1090 Vienna, Kolingasse 6* **[110 B1]***; Tel. 317 33 84*

By boat: *DDSG Blue Danube Schifffahrt; 1010 Vienna, Friedrichstrasse 7; Tel. 588 80-0; Fax 588 80-440 (May–Oct only)*

On foot: The *Vienna Guide Service; 1190 Vienna, Sommerhaidenweg 124; Tel. 440 30 94-0; Fax 440 28 25*, provides guides; half a day: approx. 100 Euro, a whole day (up to seven hours): approx. 200 Euro. A group of freelance, state-certified tourist guides has put together a programme of 'Viennese Walks' – several of them also in English – on over 60 different city themes (e.g. 'Art Nouveau', the 'Vi-

What does it cost?

Taxi	**2 Euro** per kilometre
Coffee	**2 Euro** a cup of espresso
Water	**1.40 Euro** a glass of mineral water
Wine	**2.50 Euro** a glass of wine
Bus ride	**1.50 Euro** single ticket
Snack	**approx. 2.50 Euro** a frankfurter at a hot-dog stand

ennese coffee house', and 'The Third Man') *Information: Tel. 894 53 63 and www.wienguide.at and in the free monthly guides, obtainable from Tourist Information Offices.* A similar programme is available from *Per-Pedes-Stadtführungen; Einsiedlergasse 6–8; Tel. 544 96 68.*

TAXI

Radio taxis: *Tel. 313 00; 401 00; 601 60; 814 00.* Waiting times are stated upon taking the call (generally max. ten minutes). For destinations outside the city, agree fares in advance.

TELEPHONE & CELLPHONE

Public telephones take phonecards (5 Euro, 10 Euro or 20 Euro) available from post offices and tobacconist's. Rates vary according to the time of day. Phoning from hotels, restaurants and other public buildings is generally more expensive than from a phone box or post office. Cellphone rates differ greatly according to provider, time of day and tariff. The international dialling code for Vienna is 00431; for Britain dial 0044, for the USA and Canada 001.

THEATRE TICKETS

If possible, order tickets well in advance, in writing. Staatsoper, Volksoper, Burgtheater und Akademietheater: *Bundestheaterverband; 1010 Vienna, Hanuschgasse 3* [110 C5]*; Tel. 514 44-0.* Other theatres, musicals, festivals *Vienna Ticket Service; Börsegasse 1* [110 C1–2]*; Tel. 534 17-0; Mon–Fri 9 am–5 pm;* pop and rock concerts and other major events: *Österreich Ticket Express; Tel. 960 96 (Mon to Sat 9 am–9 pm, Sun 10 am–9 pm);* collect tickets in both cases from *Kaufhaus Steffl, Kärntner Strasse 13; 3rd floor* [111 D4]*; Mon–Fri 9.30 am–7 pm, Sat 9.30 am–5 pm.* Theater an der Wien, Ronacher, Raimundtheater and other events listed by the *Vienna Events Service (WVS): Wien-Ticket; credit card ticket orders: Tel. 588 85 (daily 9 am–9 pm).*

TIME ZONES

Austria is six hours ahead of US Eastern Standard Time and one hour ahead of Greenwich Mean Time.

TIPPING

In restaurants and other gastronomic establishments, round up the bill by between 5 and 10 per cent, depending on how satisfied you were with the service. Smaller bonuses are customary for taxi drivers and hairdressers. Room service staff at the hotel usually expect 1–2 Euro (per day); filling station attendants and porters between 50 cents and 1.50 Euro.

Weather in Vienna

	Jan	Feb	Mar	Apr	May	June	July	Aug	Sept	Oct	Nov	Dec
Daytime temperatures in °C/°F	1/34	3/37	8/48	14/57	19/66	22/72	25/77	24/75	20/68	14/57	7/45	3/37
Night-time temperatures in °C/°F	–4/25	–2/28	1/34	6/43	10/50	13/55	15/59	15/59	11/52	7/45	3/37	–1/30
Sunshine: hours per day	2	3	4	6	7	8	8	8	7	5	2	1
Rainfall: days per month	8	7	8	8	9	9	9	9	7	8	8	8

Street Atlas of Vienna

Please refer to the back cover for an overview
of this Street Atlas

Thanks to

Autobahn Motorway		Autoroute Autosnelweg
Vierspurige Straße Road with four lanes		Route à quatre voies Weg met vier rijstroken
Durchgangsstraße Thoroughfare		Route de transit Weg voor doorgaand verkeer
Hauptstraße Main road		Route principale Hoofdweg
Sonstige Straßen Other roads		Autres routes Overige wegen
Fußgängerzone Pedestrian zone		Zone piétonne Voetgangerszone
Information Information	**i**	Information Information
Parkplatz - "Park + Ride" Parking place - "Park and Ride"	P P+R	Parking - "Park + Ride" Parkeerplaats - "Park + Ride"
Hauptbahn mit Bahnhof Main railway with station		Chemin de fer principal avec gare Belangrijke spoorweg met station
Sonstige Bahn Other railway		Autre ligne Overige spoorweg
Straßenbahn - Buslinie Tramway - Bus-route		Tramway - Ligne d'autobus Tram - Buslijn
Anlegestelle - Fährlinie Landing stage - Ferry line	⚓	Embarcadère - Ligne de bac Aanlegplaats - Veerdienst
Kirche - Ochenswerte Kirche Church - Church of interest		Église - Église remarquable Kerk - Bezienswaardige kerk
Polizeistation - Postamt Police station - Post office	● ✉	Poste de police - Bureau de poste Politiebureau - Postkantoor
Krankenhaus - Denkmal Hospital - Monument	✚ ⚱	Hôpital - Monument Ziekenhuis - Monument
Hotel - Jugendherberge Hotel - Youth hostel	**H** ▲	Hôtel - Auberge de jeunesse Hotel - Jeugdherberg
Campingplatz Camping site	⚕	Terrain de camping Kampeerterrein
Bebauung, öffentliches Gebäude Built-up area, public building		Zone bâtie, bâtiment public Woongebied, openbaar gebouw
Industriegelände Industrial area		Zone industrielle Industrieterrein
Park, Wald - Weinberg Park, forest - Vineyard		Parc, bois - Vignoble Park, bos - Wijnberg
Stadtgrenze Municipal boundary		Limite municipale Stadsgrens
Stadtspaziergänge Walking tours		Promenades en ville Wandelingen door de stad

D

Schloßhofer
Str.

Schliemann-G.

Franklin-

E

F

Donaufelder

Donaufelder

500 m

3

26

Str.

FLORIDSDORF

XXI.

Freiligrath-
platz

Rautenkranz-

gasse

Nordmann-

Nordmann-

An

der

Schanze

An der S

An

Donau

gasse

An

ALTE DONAU

Eisenbahnerbad

Weg

Drygalski-

der

Arbeiter-
strandbad

Arbeiterstrandbad-

Str.

Donauturm-

Städt
Strandbad
"Alte Donau"

Bundessportbad

Taxi

Donauturm

P

Seehühn.

Iriasee

DONAU-
STADT

Donaupark

Sportanlage
der ÖBB

Alte Donau

U

Rade-
bucht

XXII.

Str.

Tennis-
pl.

Bernstein-

Leuchard-

Austria Center Vienna

UNO- City

(Vienna International Centre)

Taxi

4

Vienna Int. Centre

Donau
City

Bruno-
Kreisky-
Platz

8

Nausch-
gasse

Taxi

Jul.- Payer-
G.

Donau- City-
Str.

Kaiserm.-
Vienna Int. Centre

U B

Kaiserwasser

Bootsverleih

Wagramer

Weissau-

Kl. Säufenhaufen

Sp.

3

Wien-
Reichsbrücke

Schüttau

KAISER-
MÜHLEN

6

tenbf.

Donau-
insel

U

115

119

8

Reichs-
brücke

Rudolf

Ernst-
Sadil-
Pl.

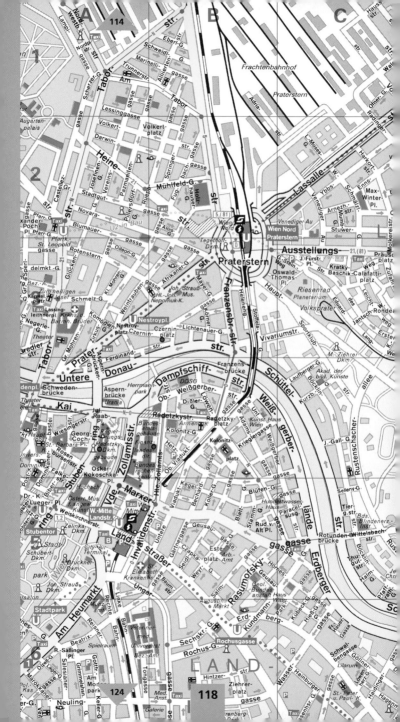

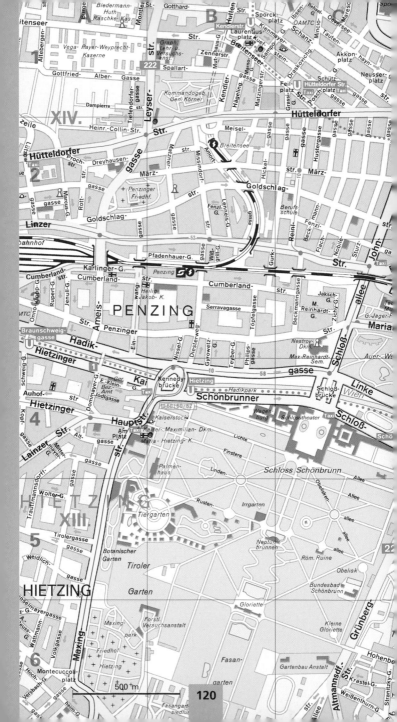

STREET ATLAS INDEX

This index lists a selection of the streets and squares shown in the Street Atlas

This index lists all sights, important terms and persons featured in this guide. Numbers in bold indicate a main entry, italics a photograph.

Get in touch!

Dear reader,

We make every effort to ensure you get the most up-to-date information available for your trip. Although our authors have done their research very carefully, errors or omissions do sometimes occur. We regret that the publisher cannot be held responsible for the consequences of such mistakes. We do, however, look forward to receiving your comments.

Please write to the editorial team at MARCO POLO Redaktion, Mairs Geographischer Verlag, Postfach 31 51, 73751 Ostfildern, Germany; or via e-mail: marcopolo@mairs.de

Picture credits

Cover photograph: Prater (Huber: Gräfenhain)
Photos: R. Hackenberg (12, 58, 88); HB Verlag (2 top, 78, 83); HB Verlag: Krause (flap, cover right, 1, 5 left, 7, 11, 16, 17, 18, 20, 28, 41, 44, 50, 60, 90, 94, 99); Hotel Imperial (73); Huber: Gräfenhain (107); L. Janicek (39); G. Jung (cover left, cover centre, 4, 19, 36, 61, 100); J. Kalmar (2 bottom, 47, 66, 84); laif: Huber (54, 97); Mauritius: Bernhaut (92), Cash (9, 68), de Kord (31, 40), Krinninger (25), Matassa (5 right, 24), Müller (35), Waldkirch (86); ÖFVW (29); P. Trummer (6)

1st edition 2004 © Mairs Geographischer Verlag, Ostfildern, Germany
4th (11th) revised German edition
Editorial director: Ferdinand Ranft, Chief editor: Marion Zorn, Editor: Manfred Pötzscher
Picture editor: Gabriele Forst, Editor English edition: Marlis von Hessert-Fraatz, Translator: Jane Riester
Cartography for the Street Atlas: © Mairs Geographischer Verlag/Falk Verlag, Ostfildern, Germany
Design and layout: red.sign, Stuttgart

BMGF - BUNDESMINISTERIUM
NEAR PLANETARIUM

Do's and don'ts

**Vienna also has its tourist traps
and things it's best to avoid**

Forgetting to leave a tip
The baksheesh principle may call to mind the derogatory comment made in some quarters that Vienna is the gateway to the Balkans. The custom of tipping is seen here more in terms of 'live and let live'. The fact is that waiters, taxi drivers, hairdressers, filling station and lavatory attendants rely heavily on such gifts to make ends meet.

Sightseeing with your own car and parking illegally
Traffic jams and too few parking spaces are notorious problems in the centre of Vienna. Forget the car. Most sights are within walking distance and the public transport network is densely woven. EU tourists will find that ignored parking tickets are rigorously pursued across national borders. If your vehicle is obstructing traffic, you can only retrieve it after paying a fine of 170 Euro. Those caught 'in the act' generally come off cheaper, especially if they pay on the spot rather than wait for the official notice to arrive by post.

Following the crowds to the Heuriger
Don't make the mistake of going to the Grinzing wine tavern with the long queue of tourist coaches parked outside! A visit to a Heuriger demands a certain amount of intimacy to be truly appreciated. Choose one of the others – you won't regret it.

Ordering 'coffee'
In the classic coffee houses of Vienna, you'll do yourself no favours if you order a simple 'Kaffee', even if the waiter doesn't bat an eyelid! Here, if you please, it is customary to order a 'Brauner' (with milk) or a 'Schwarzer' (without), a 'Kapuziner' (with a dash of cream), a 'Melange' (half milk, half coffee) ...

Dressing too casually for the opera
The majority of Vienna's culture-vultures don what they consider 'suitable attire' for their evening at the theatre. To you and me, that means, no mini-skirts, no T-shirts, no jeans or, heaven forbid, shorts! For gentlemen, jackets and ties are a must.

Dodging fares
However tempting it may seem, don't travel without paying. Be warned! The 'Schwarzkappler' (black caps) do indeed patrol the buses, trams and U-Bahn trains, and those they catch without a ticket pay an on-the-spot fine of 40 Euro; in the S-Bahn it's as much as 70 Euro.